FAST

75 ESSAYS OF FLASH NONFICTION

FALLEN

WOMEN

EDITED BY GINA BARRECA

FAST FALLEN WOMEN

75 ESSAYS OF FLASH NONFICTION

EDITED BY GINA BARRECA

Woodhall Press | Norwalk, CT

woodhall press

Woodhall Press, 81 Old Saugatuck Road, Norwalk, CT 06855
WoodhallPress.com
Copyright © 2023 Regina Barreca

Cover design: Kelsey Tynik
Layout artist: L.J. Mucci

Library of Congress Cataloging-in-Publication Data available

ISBN 978-1-954907-78-2   (paper: alk paper)
ISBN 978-1-954907-79-9   (electronic)

First Edition
Distributed by Independent Publishers Group
(800) 888-4741

Printed in the United States of America

Contents

Contents

Contents

Contents

Contents

Writing it down is the opposite of covering it up. The seventy-five pieces in this collection see large subjects through small lenses, as all writers of short pieces must. But their attention to detail must not be mistaken for an appetite for minutiae. All good writing reflects and illuminates life; *Fast Fallen Women* holds up a compact mirror. You might well see yourself.

Introduction

Let your hair down.
Let your clothes fall to the floor.
Fall for a line.
Fall in value.
Fall on your back, fall on your knees, fall into the gutter.
And look up. Sigh, heal, laugh, understand. Then rise.

The fallen woman is in motion. She has a story. She's usually kept it to herself. Not here. Through memoir, confession, humor, lived experience, professional discoveries, and intimate revelations, *Fast Fallen Women* gives whispered conversations a full voice.

Without fallen women, where would we be? Let's start their literary history with motherless Eve in Eden, head through Milton in *Paradise Lost*, get into Kate from *Taming of the Shrew* (or Juliet in *Romeo and Juliet*, for that matter, who, as we recall, has sex with one man then dies), and swerve through Austen's *Lady Susan* (and all the bitchy women in the rest of Austen's books, not ignoring Austen herself, who once described the stillbirth of a neighbor's child as occurring because the child happened to look at its father unawares), until we encounter the ur-fallen-woman of the modern era—1847, to be precise—Becky Sharp in Thackery's *Vanity Fair*, be shocked still by Scarlett O'Hara in the Pulitzer Prize–winning (if racist) *Gone with the Wind*, see the success of Loos's preferred blonde in Lorelei (who refuses to fall but can be pushy), learn what happens to women of color who also refuse to fall in Hurston's *Their Eyes Were Watching God*, meet Gloria Wandrous, who literally falls in *BUtterfield 8*, see what happens to young women who might not fall but who wobble in Plath's *The Bell Jar*, give sidelong glances at the girl who is all of age twelve at the beginning of Vladimir Nabokov's *Lolita*, glimpse the emergence of women who engineer their falls for fun in Jong's *Fear of Flying*, witness what punishments might happen to women who enjoy their falls too much if word gets around in Atwood's *The Handmaid's Tale*, learn how women triumph over their falls in Morrison's *Beloved*, and celebrate the rise of women of Zadie Smith's *White Teeth*. And that only takes us up to the start of the last century.

To get anywhere, a woman must fall. You can fall by being tipsy, getting ahead of yourself, by missing a step. You can fall because there was a blind alley, a sharp curve, a slippery surface, or a stumbling block. You fall because somebody pulls the rug out from under you or because the whole time as you stood, believing you were on solid ground, there was a trapdoor directly beneath you.

You might swoon, faint, trip, trip up, or get swept off your feet. You may be dumped, discarded, disregarded, been used up, or have been of no particular value in the first place.

You can fall because you were abandoned and then became a woman of abandon. Consider the word "abandon": If you're abandoned, you're left behind, you're emptied out; something or someone else comes in, the way it would into an abandoned building that was vacated and ripe for the next tenant.

But a woman of abandon? That's something else. That's where you've said, "I'm done. I'm not paying attention to what you told me, to all those rules telling me how I'm supposed to stay stable and good."

And a woman who does something with abandon? It's almost the same, but it has to do with something positive, not negative: It's not just the release from restraint but the embrace of appetite. As if in reply to the sanctity of scarcity, she rejoices in the belief in abundance, in the idea that there is enough, or at least enough for now—and who knows what tomorrow will bring.

"Culpa" may mean "fall," but it implies responsibility. A culpable woman is a capable woman, and an admission of guilt is the price of admission into a life of free will.

As soon as you feel your own desire, you fall. To feel deeply is to fall far. The fallen woman is controlling or out of control; she is out for herself or out of her mind; she is out for blood and out of bounds. A fallen woman is a dangerous woman because she has nothing left to lose.

Think of this collection of essays as a companion. Fallen women are often used as an object lesson, as the subject of a tutorial on how not to become her. This book is no such tutorial; it is a celebration. It encourages you to take risks. The risk of failure, rejection, humilia-tion—the risk of losing place for yourself entirely and not being able to get it back, of being seen as foolish, brazen, bitchy, grabby, and batshit crazy. Embrace the fall.

Here's to every woman who lost her virginity
but kept the box it came in.

Here's to every woman who felt she was the *only* girl who wasn't
pure, perfect, and upright.

And Mom, here's to you: You were not a bad girl.
You were simply ahead of your time.

Party Girl

by MAGGIE MITCHELL

I want, I want, I want, I wrote in my diary when I was sixteen. Teenage life was supposed to resemble a John Hughes film, I imagined, and in the *Breakfast Club* of my dreams, I wanted to be Molly Ringwald—the party-girl princess, not the freak or the brain. I'd convinced myself that my classmates were living a small-town version of this life, and that some flaw in my character excluded me from their world of cars, dates, parties, laughter—a flaw as solid and insurmountable as a wall.

Or maybe it wasn't my character; maybe it was just my image: bookish, four-eyed, tongue-tied—"square," in '80s parlance. So I set out to rectify that. I acquired contact lenses, had my hair cut, spent my babysitting money on clothes, dusted my eyelids with blue shadow. I made the cheerleading squad.

The wall wavered a bit—but there it still stood.

So when the one friend who had stuck by me since kindergarten suggested that we get drunk before a school dance, it seemed like a perfect opportunity to deliver a deathblow to my spotless reputation. Classmates had been chugging vodka or rum from soda bottles on bus trips since we were thirteen. I had disapproved. Uninvited, I had also envied. Maybe they'd had the right idea all along? I had no reason to think so: I was no stranger to drunken adults; I should have known that drinking was not the magical path to happiness.

Still, had the woman who agreed to procure us booze bought wine coolers, as we requested, the night might have ended differently. Instead she purchased a bottle of MD 20/20, or Mad Dog—more bang for our babysitting bucks, she explained! It was sticky and sweet and didn't hit me right away. So I kept drinking.

For me, dances had always been desperate, solitary affairs, though I attended them religiously. This one, I vowed, would be different.

And so it must have been. Memory serves up only disconnected, strobe-lit snapshots: I am dancing with unthinkable abandon. I am hiding in the girls' restroom. I'm struggling to extricate myself from a bin of winter coats. I'm sitting in the front hallway of my own house, alone. I'm in the guidance counselor's office, fluorescent lights beating down. *I don't know where my mother is*, I'm insisting. I'm at a teacher's house, collapsing onto a pullout couch. My mother is threatening to kill me. The teacher and her husband hover in their bathrobes, protective.

Between the snapshots, blank space, as in an old photo album.

I pieced the story together later: My friend escorted me home but a chaperone followed, dragged me back to school. An ambulance came. I declined to have my stomach pumped. Unable to reach my mother, someone called a teacher.

By morning I was the talk of the town—the coffee shop, the bar, the post office.

At a hearing to determine whether I (the presumptive valedictorian) should be kicked out of the National Honor Society, character witnesses spoke on my behalf; a classmate's mother testified against me, as did my Civics teacher. Rules are rules, they said. My mother sat silently beside me, simmering with rage. I was merely suspended. I was banned from dances, sentenced to detention.

My diary is cryptic on the subject: *I have something to tell you—it's major . . . and it's bad.* The entry stops there. At fifteen, I had documented the books I read and dissected my loneliness. By sixteen I'd traded *The Bell Jar* for *Sixteen Candles*. I cataloged my triumphs: got drunk at a dance, went to a party, kissed a boy. By the end of the year, the dance earned only a mention as one in a long list of dubious social milestones.

But the diary is a careful fiction. It omits my mother's disgust, the brutal humiliation of the hearing. Friends overheard their parents wondering if I should go to rehab. Kind teachers mortified me by asking if there was trouble at home, if I wanted to talk. But: *1986 was a successful experiment*, I wrote breezily.

"I'm not the girl you think I am," I had wanted to announce. But—who was I, then? Someone who could screw up, lose control, let people down? That was not what I had meant to say. And it was not something I could bear to know.

So I constructed a new wall, and behind it I entombed my shame, too molten and poisonous for words.

Lousy Dancer

by CAROLINE LEAVITT

I'm twenty-four and in the Pittsburgh ballet studio shaking with sweat. But not just because of the four pirouettes I've struggled to do, but because I'm terrified someone in class knows my secret—that my marriage to a handsome, brilliant attorney is shattering; and because of that, I'm having a torrid affair with the fifty-plus ballet teacher, who is bald, denture-wearing, trailer park–living, married, and about to have a baby with his wife.

What the hell am I doing?

I always come early to the studio and leave late, a ballet addiction that soothes my desperate need to focus on anything other than my husband seeming to hate me. I spend hours talking with our instructor. "The gnome," the other women call him, which he truly is, but when he talks to me—about dance, about photography, about life and writing—he makes me feel truly seen, interesting and important. I don't just look forward to our talks, I need them; and to my surprise, I fall heedlessly into love and it's glorious. But I can't tell him that to his face.

Instead, I tell him with anonymous hand-painted-by-me cards. "You make my heart do a grand jeté," I write. Corny. Unforgivable. But effective, because in class, he asks, "Who is sending me these wonderful cards?" The other women joke, "You did it! No, you!" I radiate joy and say nothing.

He invites me to his trailer park to meet his family. And, oh my God, I go. His pregnant wife is kind and sets out a spread; his kids are funny and smart, but he leaves me alone with his children while he and his wife go outside to "have a discussion," and they come back subdued. And when he drives me home, he leans toward me and kisses me, and I don't fall apart until I am back in my silent, husband-empty apartment. I don't have to ask what I'm doing because I know: I am being saved from sorrow.

Before and after class, I kiss him. I strip out of my leotard and tights and have sex with him. The way he looks at me! We never talk about the future except that he tells me he is in love with me, and he won't leave his wife or his kids, or me.

One day, my husband tells me he might have a venereal disease. He swears he has been faithful. I burst into terrified tears but stay silent, because how can I tell him what I've been doing? The next day, I rush to ballet early to tell my teacher, and he says, thoughtfully, "Well, I've only slept with three other dancers recently." My legs go limp. I leave the class and refuse to come back, even when he begs me. Soon afterward, my husband, still clueless about my teacher, wants a divorce.

I move to Manhattan. I take ballet class for a while before I give up ballet for good, knowing it wasn't the dancing so much that drew me. It was the dance teacher. And I begin to realize that I am seeing myself differently now: I feel younger, stronger, happy, full of amazing possibilities. My writing career zooms along with my romantic life, and if the men I see don't appreciate or talk to me, *I* am the one to drop *them*. And no one has to remind me of my new blessings, because I remind myself.

I don't regret my time with my dance teacher ever, because seeing myself through his gaze finally pushed me to see myself through my own. And I began to truly like what I saw.

Fallen Woman

by AMY TAN

In November I was stepping backward to avoid rambunctious children. My foot slid off a sloped rock and I lost my balance, falling backward. Fortunately, I had on so many layers of clothes that I didn't even bruise myself. Because I instinctively extended my arm, though, I put a lot of force on my wrist and sprained it. Now I mull over how I can learn to fall without incurring damage. I have osteoporosis and turn seventy this year. The concerns are real.

Need motivation? There are alarming statistics concerning women over age sixty who suffer hip fractures from falls. One in five women will die in the first year.

Most fall-related injuries occur at home—for men, it is often from falling from heights, say, while on a ladder cleaning the gutters.

Here are my own "live and learn" lessons:

1. Always use the handrail when taking the stairs. I estimate I've fallen a half dozen times over my lifetime. Many would not have happened if I had used a handrail. Have them installed. If you think you don't need it, think about elderly friends or relatives who are not as fit as you.

2. Turn on the light when it's dark, or use an auto-on nightlight. I use one of those clip-on reading lights when heading for the bathroom if my husband is sleeping.

3. Don't carry a bunch of stuff in both hands, especially if those items block you from seeing obstacles or uneven steps.

4. Never walk while looking at your cell phone. A fire-fighter in NYC told me that one of the leading causes of

pedestrian deaths is inattention while looking at a cell phone and wearing headphones.

5. Routinely scan ahead to note obstacles or changing conditions. I once was engaged in talking to someone as we strolled on a level walkway. I did not notice that the flat walkway was becoming an elevated sidewalk with a five-inch curb. My left foot rolled off the curb and I broke my ankle. I was lucky it wasn't my hip.

6. Be aware of throw rugs. They could a real danger for those with Parkinson's or MS.

7. Consider installing grab bars in your shower and tub. My current home has teak grab bars in the bathrooms and in the guest powder room. I love their look and their usefulness.

8. Be careful when walking on marble tile. I once slipped three times in a hotel that had beautiful marble floors polished to a shine. Wear nonskid shoes with traction even on slick surfaces.

9. Be aware of dogs and cats that tend to get underfoot.

10. Get into a balanced position when stepping out of the car. I once hurriedly stepped out of the car on one foot when the door was not fully open. I exited sideways with one foot still in the car, lost my balance, had nothing to grab onto, and fell backward. I hit my head on concrete. That's one way to end your writing career. I recommend opening the door fully and swinging your legs together so that both feet are on the ground before standing up. A friend described it as "the ladylike way we were told to sit when we wore tight skirts in the '60s."

11. Slow down when walking fast and changing directions. Your required balance shifts.

12. Remove obstacles on the floor, like magazines, clothes, and charging cords. I know of one author who broke a leg when he got out of bed and immediately slid on a magazine.

13. If you go barefoot or wear only socks indoors, use grippy socks.

14. If you need to get something from up high on a shelf, use something sturdy to stand on, and know what you can hold onto if you lose your balance.

15. Think twice about using a ladder, indoors or out. My husband had a ladder slide out from under him when he was changing a light bulb on a fourteen-foot-high ceiling. He was lucky he was not killed.

16. Do core body exercises. Do stretches. Practice turning your head to the side one way and then the other. Turning your head to see something is better than turning your whole body.

17. If you have a tall bedframe, box spring, and thick mattress, consider a lower bed.

18. When wearing a long skirt or wide-legged pant, be careful not to step on the hem, especially when going up stairs. I tripped and sprained several toes this way. Lift your hem.

The Woman on the Motorcycle, Riding Alone

by MARNA DEITCH

In the early 1980s, not many women rode their own motorcycles. Motorcycling itself was only *just* becoming recognized by everyday middle-class society with the introduction of the Honda Rebel.

In the early '80s, my life was changing, and the world was changing around it.

In 1980 I was twenty-two years old. My grandfather died on April 6; April 8 was his funeral. April 10 was my grandmother's stroke. April 11 was my father's stroke; he went into a coma April 12 and died April 19. My mother died on June 8 of breast cancer. My grandmother survived her original stroke but died on April 19, 1985, the anniversary of my mother's, her baby daughter's, passing.

I was a NYC stage actor (okay, waiter), and the disease that wiped out the theater community was only beginning its then nameless assault. We learned to call it AIDS. I lost many of my closest friends. In March of 1985, one of my best friends, Gene, went out dancing with my very best friend, Kenny. After leaving a gay men's bar at closing time, around 4:00 a.m., Kenny realized he couldn't convince Gene to get into a taxi. Gene had fallen into a hypoglycemic depression and insisted on going to the Christopher Street Pier alone. What followed was a six-week search before his body floated down the Hudson River past the World Trade Center towers.

I was devastated. I was empty. I was void. Gene's lover of six years, George, who had been my date to my high school prom, felt the same way: a shell after a grueling six-week, nonstop, sleepless search.

One morning, George said to me, "You're moving to California, aren't you? Can I come with you?"

"George, I'd love that!"

"How'd you like to go by motorcycle?"

"You're crazy! Neither one of us has even been a passenger on a bike. What the hell. Oh, let's do it."

We took lessons, passed our road tests, bought bikes the next day, packed up, and left New York.

It was exhilarating. It was petrifying. We did not have enough experience. We rode south from New York to Washington, DC, and Virginia, then to West Virginia and down toward New Orleans.

We got along; we didn't get along. We rode through the Ozarks, and a group of bikers kept passing us, calling us "The Honeymooners." Both of us being gay, and George being VERY gay, we kept our awareness level at "Alert." We had agreed to tent across country, but George kept wanting to get motel rooms. We stopped talking in Texas, spent two days in a campsite in Oklahoma not talking at all. George hated being on the road. He hated camping.

What we didn't know at the time was that George was HIV positive. He was starting to weaken. We couldn't have known that. We just decided that he would stay in Texas and then go back east. I would go on alone.

I became an unusual American: I was a woman biker.

Alone, I left Texas.

I was alone that drizzly morning in October 1985. But I swear, when I crossed the border into New Mexico, the sun broke through the clouds, the rain stopped, and my mood exploded with the brightness.

I OWNED this road now. I was a WOMAN BIKER! ALONE! I felt a pride and confidence I had never felt before.

On the road, I got comments of approval from many people, especially older folks. I went alone from Texas to California, then back to New York, then up through New England into Canada, back into the

United States through Michigan, then back to California. A small newspaper in Minnesota wrote about my passing through their town. When I settled in West Hollywood, word spread about the woman who "rode cross country all alone."

I knew that the motorcycle was the most amazing life gift anyone had ever put in front of me, and it was George who had put it there, as if saying: "Your parents and grandparents are gone; Gene, Kenny, and I are gone. We're not going to be with you, but we're going to give you the chance for an amazing life." George died soon after I made that first solo ride.

I have ridden through all fifty states, including the Arctic Circle and Hawaii, all because George said, "How'd you like to go by motorcycle?"

I found the courage, which sometimes sounded like vulnerability, to say, "Oh, let's do it."

That's become my great motto: "Let's do it."

Feeling Thirty-nine

by EBONY MURPHY-ROOT

This is the last summer of my thirties. My youth is not over, not just yet, but it is rapidly wrapping up.

The two or three gray hairs near each of my temples, which had been the only ones of their kind until last autumn, have recently, and rapidly, sprouted company. The "Dark and Lovely" hair color I've used for brightness turn these new strands a dishwater shade. For a few days, they might appear as highlights, but they soon petulantly expel their magic and become dreary.

Dreary is not what I'm going for as I head into my forties. I am looking for exuberance. I'm going for unapologetic self-acceptance and celebration.

A chiropractor who treats some current and retired sports stars is always kind enough to fit me in when my hips and shoulders feel stiff. I tell myself it's because he finds me refreshing. In many respects, not including the gray hairs, I'm youthful for my age. Many people my age, I've discovered, have grandchildren. Perhaps this is not always the case in New York City or LA, but it is true in the middle of the country, or in the middle of states I don't often visit.

I do not have children or want them. For some, this might place me in the category of fallen women. I consider myself simply decisive. I also consider myself child-free, not childless. I am a Black woman, and because I am fairly good with kids and fairly educated, my lack of desire to be a mother often confounds people; it even angers a few.

It's not that I didn't listen for the possible call of maternity. When I married at twenty-eight, lots of people insisted I would suddenly want children. When I turned thirty and did not, some folks uttered two of the most bizarre statements in the English language: "Just have one and see," and "It's different when they're your own."

I am surrounded by children in my role as a teacher, mostly delightfully moody preteens on the cusp of adolescence, but they do not come home with me.

After a long day with adolescents who would rather trade finger skateboards and bid on rare, expensive sneakers than craft essays on Jason Reynolds, Adrienne Rich, Ibram X. Kendi, Naomi Shihab Nye, and Heather Cox Richardson, I do not want to wrangle my own preadolescent folks to T-ball or gymnastics. What I want is to have a glass of good Malbec and enjoy it somewhere sparsely decorated, quiet, and chic.

The bands I go see—Dave Matthews, the Indigo Girls, and The Roots—have audiences who appear to be galloping toward middle age or who are well beyond it. When I was at Jones Beach on Long Island jamming to "Two Step" with my friend Toren, I looked at the Gen Xers and very old millennials clutching giant cans of Liquid Death and Twisted Tea, and clucked to myself, "Is that what I look like?" My students listen to Jack Harlow and Billie Eilish, and the only two presidents they've known are Obama and Trump.

I never take my age for granted.

My mother was this age, thirty-nine, when she passed away of a terrible, metastatic breast cancer. I was a senior in high school looking forward to literature classes and D-1 track meets at the state school forty-five minutes away. One weekend in May was her funeral, the next was my senior prom, and the next was graduation.

One of my great sadnesses is that very few people checked in on me after the trauma of losing my mother. My high school friends considered me a drag; some even told me so. My mother's thicket of colleagues and friends seemed to disappear almost overnight. My father was a forty-four-year-old widower with three sad children who didn't think to suggest therapy or grief groups.

Then George W. Bush lost the presidential election and still got to be president, and Al Gore went off to make documentaries. The economy went to shit. I took teacher certification classes and toiled as case manager for foster kids for $14 an hour.

That was my kickoff to mother loss, adulthood, war, and recession.

So when I get to blow out the "4" and "0" candles on my cake later this year, I will take comfort in the ways I have mothered myself, and joyfully done my part for the next generation.

Someday I will get old. Not just yet.

Planned Parenthood

by DEBORAH HOCHMAN TURVEY

Thank God for planned parenthood. THANK God for Planned Parenthood. I was twenty-four when I found myself pregnant. I didn't tell my sisters or my parents, not because they would have judged me but because I was too ashamed.

I did what a young woman who felt alone in a crisis did: I called Planned Parenthood. I went into the center. I corrected a mistake without changing the course of many lives. It was legal. It was straightforward. It was not easy. I ended up calling my parents crying the next day, and they brought me home with them to recover.

My mom then told me about her abortion. I wonder if I would have felt so ashamed if I had known about it before.

Several years later I married. I was thirty when I had my first child; thirty-two when I had my first miscarriage. Two more miscarriages and two more children followed. Seven pregnancies, three miscarriages, four D&Cs, three C-sections, three children, six years of nursing.

I was fifty-two when I learned that miscarriages are not some cosmic paybacks for terminating a pregnancy. They weren't a form of punishment for being fallen, for making a mistake, for having sex. My body wasn't listening to the ancestral, patriarchal, universally controlling voice that whispered: *Your fault*. It was me whispering those terrible things to myself, holding onto emotions far longer than necessary, making connections where there were none.

It took me more than twenty-four years and a blood clot to let go of the shame that had convinced me that my miscarriages were not some karmic retributions. Like so many things, it turns out that superstition and shame are not actual influences, and they do not inform how any of this works.

Science works, and good medical care works.

The short story is that at age fifty-two, a blood clot landed me in the hospital, leading to a diagnosis for two genetic clotting disorders. That short story, however, had a long road paved with patronizing doctors and a health-care system that says women are irrational, that we exaggerate, and that we can't be trusted to tell you what's going on with our own bodies. Turns out the medical system and the judicial system are remarkably similar.

(Fuck you, Supreme Court.)

My story is that I took myself to the ER after suffering unbearably at home for two days. Initially, I had called a surgeon, but he dismissed my symptoms, telling me I'd overdone it on the Peloton and suggesting I call in the morning if I was still hurting.

I did the opposite of what women are taught to do: I ignored him. Ignoring the surgeon might have saved my life. I took myself to the hospital.

I was relieved when the resident came into the ER to tell me I had a massive blood clot in my portal vein. So convinced that my unbearable pain was somehow in my head, I remember blurting out to her, "So I'm *not* crazy"—the mantra of women all over the world.

I learned that clotting disorders can cause multiple miscarriages. Abortions can't.

Because when women whisper about their losses—both planned and unplanned—and whisper about their medical care—both planned and unplanned—the medical community, our government, and our communities silence women, not just from discussing loss and miscarriages, but also from any self-determining conversation.

We don't call the doctor, because who calls someone who doesn't listen to them?

We don't know our moms and friends also had abortions, and so we isolate and hang onto those misbeliefs, do what we have been taught to do.

We quiet our voices and smile, because we look prettier when we smile. And when that happens, there are unintended consequences.

Those consequences cause pain, they cause suffering, and they cause shame. When I started sharing my story, it turned out to not be terribly different from anyone else's. Not every abortion is related to a tragic or horrific event. Some are, make no mistake about it. But some are moments in time that we can talk about and move past. Reasons are reasons, and we each have our own. Sometimes people make mistakes, and a mistake is a mistake.

As my brilliant and compassionate father told me: "You made one mistake. Don't make two."

Good Calcium and a Red Sky

by HONOR MOORE

Fallen Woman by Louise Bourgeois (Femme Maison, 1946–47);
Metropolitan Museum of Art, June 2022

Brisk early-spring evening in New York and I trip and fall, pick myself right up, and thank my grandmother, who sent us Guernsey milk from her farm when I was a child—ridiculous, but I have good calcium.

Scratched and bruised shin, a little blood. I'll act as if it didn't happen.

The artist is known for her sculpture, odd shapes, very "female." I met her once, or was it that I once saw a really good portrait photograph? She died in 2010, and these are paintings she made between 1938 and 1949: She is developing her imagery. A rectangular painting hangs horizontal, six feet long, three wide, an eccentrically conceived figure of a woman reclining, suspended in a red sky. Blood red: *Fallen Woman*.

Fallen but also aloft. Across the middle of her abdomen, a dark gray likeness of a tenement block. Lights on.

By the time I started to have sex, the idea of a fallen woman was obsolete. The sexual revolution had pulled the fallen woman up from the ground. We wanted to have sex, all of us. I sought that dimension, sky, view of heaven. When our moment began, we didn't know about orgasm: What is this lofting jolt, this shock infusing viscera with spirit, taking the body with it?

When a woman in her seventies falls on a city street, she feels like a tree falling. A tall self, falling over. The moments she arcs downward, *Will I break?*

When she is upright, when you are upright, when I am upright; walking, and the shoe catches on the cement curb. Careen, fall, a hard landing. Because I have good calcium, I did not break myself. I have never broken myself, a curse to say it.

A taint of accusation hovers when I write about sexuality: She has had bad relationships, they say. Fallen woman, the woman who sins, adulteress, slut, a stitch dropped from the fabric of society.

I didn't sleep with him, she said. I wanted him to marry me, and a man like that will not marry a woman he beds before marriage.

Sure, I'll sleep with you, but divorce your wife first, she told him. He did, and they're married still.

I identified with Mary Magdalene, the first fallen woman in my life. I wasn't interested in the Virgin in pale blue and white, sitting there with a baby on her lap. I wanted the red and purples of Magdalene, even the ravages, as in the sculpture of her in the Florence duomo, carved from wood by Donatello, haggard.

She had fallen into pleasure, too much ice cream. The smooth textures of ice cream, gelato, a bath of pleasure, and that moment of transcendence. "In his face I saw the face of God," says my friend, a poet, of his long-dead lover.

It is God I call for; I also call for God when I apprehend perfection—a tree, a mountain, a view, a lake, touching the impossibly smooth skin of an infant. Ineffable.

She is fallen only in the imagination of the patriarchs, who turn away from her humanness, deny their own. Does a man fail patriarchy when he allows himself a woman's tenderness?

We were children, two white bodies in a college room, Mahler on the record player; we were mining each other, we fell together, we shook and cried out, we clung to each other, we laughed, and we were frightened and delighted.

After that he didn't know what to do, so he ceased speaking to me.

Falling into red, of the crimson ceremony of blood, the red of Hester's A bursting its strictures, a circle of women talking. Healing, by which is not meant reentry into polite society; with the ones raped and maligned, the fallen woman holds and shares.

I reject her composure. I call for the vividness of her beauty, I call for wisdom and the body's pleasure, I call for the red shriek of her transcendence.

I can't stay in the power of that red for too long, as I must sing or weep or lie down on the floor. She flies a sky of red. The *Fallen Woman* title is a little joke. My eyes are her eye, drawn by the woman I may once have met, but perhaps I met her only in that photographic portrait.

No, I see her in black; I reach for her hand as friends introduce us.

Breaking Ground

by PAMELA KATZ

I grew up in the limbo of the Upper West Side of Manhattan in the 1970s. Religion had been rejected but not replaced; conventional morality was scoffed at without offering a substitute, and falling, like failing, was either prevented, cushioned, or utterly denied.

I was given the freedom to defy tradition and make my own rules. But as a teenager, all I wanted were rules to break.

Sensing that nature would provide the gravity I needed, I went on physically challenging summer trips. Mountains and weather were tantalizingly formidable and unforgiving.

On the first adventure, our twenty-one-year-old leader slipped on a mountain trail in New Hampshire and fell to his death. The following summer, a teenage boy from our group took a bad fall in the Rocky Mountains, landed in a glacier lake, and broke his arm.

The fact that I went on a third trip is an indication of how much I craved a world with concrete consequences, where failing meant injury or death and succeeding meant I had earned my place on Earth.

That summer, in the Olympic Mountains of Washington State, our group came upon a mountain pass that was unexpectedly snowed in. We should have turned around, but our young leader said we could slide down on our rain ponchos.

If I'd trusted myself, I would have felt a warning in my uncontrollable trembling. *Turn around. This is dangerous. You don't have to prove anything to anyone.* Instead, I heard: *You're a coward and a weakling. Everyone will laugh at you.*

I watched the others gliding down the snow on their asses, their loud "hurrahs" echoing at the bottom. I finally pushed off with eyes squeezed shut in terror, the last to go.

I spun out of control, tumbling over onto my back. I went most of the way headfirst, with the snow blowing in my face and obscuring all else. I passed out when I crashed into the trees at the bottom of the mountain.

Falling is nothing like what you see in the movies or even in your dreams. You don't glide through the air, move in slow motion, or get a glimpse of heaven.

It's more like a general anesthetic—one minute the needle goes in and, seemingly, the next second, you open your eyes and it's over.

I woke up at the bottom with a shocking pain in my leg. I screamed; everyone stared down at me in horror.

I waited three hours in the mercifully numbing snow for the helicopter to find us on the steep hillside. The medics put my leg in an air splint and lifted me into a stretcher. To my surprise, they hoisted it onto the exterior rails, and we took off. Just like an episode in *M.A.S.H.*, I was flown to safety staring up at the blades of the chopper with the wind whipping my face.

At the tiny hospital, a surreally named Dr. Nixon told me I'd broken my femur and five ribs and needed five stitches in my head. Three months in traction, one in a body cast, three in a leg cast. I missed the fall of my junior year of high school.

My broken leg healed to be an inch shorter than my left. Forty-eight years later, I can trace almost every muscular and joint ailment to that one little inch.

Recently, a masseuse began to work on the bump where my femur had healed. I told her not to bother; it was bone and would never change.

She corrected me: It was a mass of muscle that had built up around the fused bone to protect it. No longer necessary, she added, and the tense muscles were actually doing more harm than good.

I'd grown up around the break in my mind as well, convinced that surviving nature as a sixteen-year-old girl had made me adventurous, independent, and strong—the qualities my mother hoped to instill by removing the conventions that had hemmed in her generation. Without a moral compass of my own, I was like a ghost passing through walls, seeking hard surfaces in the hopes that hitting the ground would make me feel whole.

Because I'd never understood the falseness of my quest, I'd never properly healed. The scab of pretense had remained as if it could still protect me. I tear it off now, determined to remain standing in the face of life's inevitable misfortunes, rather than purposely finding a mountaintop from which to leap.

Looking Up

by JANE SMILEY

Oh, I'm sorry. When I read the title, I thought it was *Fast Falling Women*. That reminded me of when I was four and my friend down the street would run down the stairs while I held the rail and went down, right foot, right foot, right foot while everyone by the front door sighed and waited. Nothing scares me quite so much as the thought of falling down the stairs. Rewrite *King Lear*? Why not? Include as much sex as possible in a literary novel? Ah, it could get banned! That would feed the purse pocket! Stand up in front of a large audience? If I take my glasses off, I can't see them anyway, except the guy in the front row who's already fallen asleep. Four husbands? A good number, and all of them sweetie pies, especially the one who runs up and down a twelve-foot ladder without holding on. Ride a horse? One of my horses likes going downstairs. But wait, I'll be down in a minute—I have to hold both railings and stare at my feet.

Ah! The blessings of ADD! I wasn't diagnosed with attention deficit disorder when I was a kid, but I know I had it. I was restless, often yawned in class or looked out the window, and my fourth-grade teacher wrote on my report card: "She only does what she wants to do." If you have ADD, you only notice what you want to do, too, and all those instructions about how to behave, how to be a proper woman, how to dress, how to eat, and where to turn right go in one ear and out the other. Therefore, you wear what is comfortable, you yawn without covering your mouth, you stare out the window at the birds during algebra class, you find your own ideal boyfriend and pull him out of his lonely room, and you often get lost, thereby discovering all sorts of new sights, sounds, and environments. One of my inner dialogues has always been: "I'm tired. I should go home. What's that? Could be something interesting. Well, it's not far. Let's try it."

A couple months ago, I went up a trail that I thought would be easy. I got almost to the top, but it was so steep that even though I saw the end, I turned around, and went carefully back the way I had come. When I got to a part that wasn't as steep, I slipped on a pebble and fell down anyway. My left knee and hip bent backward, and I scraped my elbow—one of my worst fears realized. Except that once I managed to use a tree branch to hoist myself up, I was absolutely pain-free. *Ah,* I thought, *I can give up my fears!* Except I didn't. The next day, when I hiked a simpler trail, I couldn't stop wondering whether the price of helicoptering me to the hospital—should I fall on my face, go over the cliff, be attacked by a cougar—would be a hundred thousand dollars. My husband says that it is covered by Medicare. But even so . . .

I guess I will accept these fears as a sort of necessary background noise that I can't get rid of, that has made me cautious and observant walking, driving, and riding a horse. But as I get older and the world around us seems to be collapsing, I sometimes wonder if I should go ahead, let go of the railing, and topple head over heels down the stairs. I can imagine it—looking at my feet, looking out the window at the tree limbs rustling in the twilight breeze, thinking how beautiful it is, and then feeling my heel catch on the step; falling to the right, trying to grab the railing, my hand slipping; then rolling, hitting my shoulder, crying out; seeing my husband's face looking over the railing; rolling further, hitting my head, everything going black—disappearing bit by bit, even the sound of my husband's voice and his feet on the steps. Then nothing. Well, not a bad way to go, after all.

25

Bruce Whore

by KELLY ANDREWS-BABCOCK

I'm a Bruce Whore. Bruce Springsteen, that is.

Earning the title "Bruce Whore" is a simple matter of living, loving, and doing all things Bruce. You quote song lyrics, say things like "My car runs on Bruce." In front of your principal, you decide to go to a second concert that week instead of Family Night without remorse.

How do you get to be a Bruce Whore?

You know you're a Bruce Whore when . . .

- You're in TJ Maxx, Bruce comes on, and you start calling out, "Bruuuuuuuuccccccce!" Your teenage daughter hides, but she'll sing along in the car.
- Your colleague does a double take at the Bruce shrine behind your desk.
- You pull in for a book club meeting and the Buggy next to yours—the other Bruce Whore's—is sporting a license plate holder that says, "The only boss I listen to is Bruce," and has the same Bruce song playing.
- You give a twenty-four-year-old friend weekly Wednesday Bruce lessons.
- You see a Bruce cover band and all you can say is, "Well, thank God we never have to do that again."

There's more.

You know you're a Bruce Whore when at a U2 show in Philly, Bono calls a friend up on stage. You turn to the other Bruce Whore jumping up and down, holding hands and screaming, "Now we can die happy, to see Bruce and Bono together!" When you take road trips to Asbury Park, back to Philly to visit the Bruce Museum, reminiscing and searching for his boots—those sexy boots.

You know you're a Bruce Whore when driving to Jersey for a weekend of shows, you read a Bruce book aloud: "You've just seen the heart-stomping, ass-whooping, hard-rocking earth-shaking, booty-shaking, love-making, history-making, Viagra-taking, legendary E Street Band!" When your decisions on which T-shirt to wear are always a challenge—the black one where he's showing off his muscled triceps or the white one where he's squatting down in those damned boots?

Life can be terribly demanding.

You know you're a Bruce Whore when you stand in line for hours to get a wristband to see if you'll be in the front of the pit or not. When once you make it in and fight your way to the front of the stage—there's no turning back. When beside you on the catwalk, Bruce is kneeling, wailing on his guitar and YOU are touching his leg! Did you know he has quilted knee pads under those jeans? Yup, that's what makes the slide doable. When the next day you get a call from a parent who says, "I saw you on the screen last night, right next to Bruce!"

Part of being a Bruce Whore is admiration for the rest of the band. When Clarence played at the Wolf Den, you threw rose petals at him, tossed a scarf on stage, and bowed to him when you got his autograph—and then went back the next night.

After Clarence died, you were in mourning. In true Bruce fashion, he included a brass section of six players to replace the Big Man. Clarence's tribute was in the middle of "Tenth Avenue Freeze-Out" after the line "And the Big Man joined the band. ..." Complete silence from the band for a solid two minutes while pictures of Clarence shone and everyone sang "Clarence" and cried. Eventually on that tour, you heard the song you thought you'd never hear live again: "Jungleland." Jakey made his Uncle Clarence proud!

Bruce's music has healing power. *The Rising* followed the 9/11 tragedy with strength and resilience. Bruce helped you cope with lines like "Rise up!" while "Mary's Place" lifted you to a place of hope. There were healing shows after more difficult personal times too. A month after the Other Whore's father died, when you heard the song "Sandy," it sustained her. You laughed and cried with her, remembering how her dad warned you about going to the Big City to see Bruce. When weeks after your heart surgery, you were tailgating with your traditional rotisserie chicken, cheese, wine, and laughter prior to standing for hours singing. When you still get shivers when you hear Bruce's harmonica play the opening bars to "Thunder Road."

Soon enough, the Other Whore will be back on two cell phones, an iPad, and a desktop to find tickets and you'll be road tripping. In the meantime, you just ". . . roll down the window and let the wind blow back your hair."

Platitudes

by DARIEN HSU GEE

I love that you think you know me.

This is not a judgment. I've been guilty of it myself, looking at a woman and thinking I know her whole story. The way she dresses, how tight her clothes, how much cleavage, the fake/not-fake jewelry, flats or heels, mani/pedi. There's her makeup (or lack of). Her boobs, her ass, her toned/untoned arms. How her eye skims the room when an alpha male walks in, how it flicks away when someone less important appears. The enthusiasm (or lack of) in her voice. That expensive (or cheap) haircut. The way she shakes your hand, that smile (or lack of), that sparkle (or lack of) in her eye.

Maybe it's a rumor—someone heard she's getting a divorce. How she cheated or was cheated on. Her meds. How many graduate degrees, house and summer house, condo or vacation rental. She has/has not met Michelle Obama. She does/does not drive a Tesla. Her kids do/do not talk to her. She does/does not have a personal trainer, walks/runs five miles a day, was/was not seen gorging on doughnuts and chocolate croissants at the local bakery then crying as she stuffed the empty bag/box in the trash. Too much/not enough therapy. She is/is not broke. She is/is not alone.

But enough about me, let's talk about you. What do you think of me?
I'm kidding.
(Not kidding.)
Let's not point fingers. We did/did not think about leaving our families more than once. We may have thought/not thought about causing bodily harm to our spouse/child/neighbor/stranger on the street. The lighter/darker thoughts are saved for ourselves.

Am I ADHD, bipolar II, or just really intense and interesting?

Class reunions are the worst, don't you think? I haven't gone to mine. What face to put on? Which story to tell?

The body keeps the score; your body is a map. Have you forgotten the six-inch keloid scar across your gut—a necessary/unnecessary traumatic C-section for child #1? Birth plan -> window. Recovery: two months. PTSD/PPD, diagnosed after the fact. What kind of mother doesn't attach to her child? How about the kind of mother whose milk doesn't quite come in, who nurses for five years from guilt, who said she'd never give birth again but then had two more, the last one at home. Then there's the scar on your forehead—a fall on a dock by a lake in Denver. Or maybe it was in someone's backyard, or the cement sidewalk in front of your house. *Kersplat.* Your brother cried when he saw you; there was blood everywhere. It was very dramatic. Your head in your mother's lap, or maybe she was driving and you were in the back seat by yourself, your eight-year-old hand pressing the dish towel to your face. The doctor who blew his surgical glove into a balloon and drew a smiley face on it. Don't forget the chemistry experiment gone wrong = a second-degree burn on your left index finger. The chronic athlete's foot on one big toe. Your bad knees. Heavy periods, enlarged uterus, belly fat. Insomnia. Waking in the mornings with clenched fists.

It's disappointing, isn't it? You/I know better. You/I are well educated. There is no excuse for your very bad day. Put "bad" in air quotes, because there are others who have it worse. You have nothing to complain about. Life is what you make of it, and this mess is all yours.

Mine mine mine mine mine.

Asking/waiting/needing permission is overrated. Approval is overrated. We may not know much, but that much we know.

You are/are not a bad daughter/wife/mother. You are/are not smart enough. Why can't you write faster/sell another book/get an advance to help your kids go to college? You're good, but not good enough. You're a sellout, in it only for the money while every else writes with integrity and passion and gives back to the writing community. You are the odd woman/writer out.

Is this where you/I say we don't care anymore?

(I think so.)

The scale has tipped. You/I have crested into the back end of life. There are years left, but if you/I were planning to do something/make a mark/coast into retirement, time is not on our side. This is not to say some/more/all of it can't be done/accomplished/experienced. This is not to say you have/have not been enough. There is time, just not a lot.

What are you going to do? What are we waiting for?

You know me.

The Other Woman

by GINA BARRECA

She's the nicest woman you could ever meet. In fact, you probably have met her. You might know her fairly well, and you might like her without being aware, of course, that she's sleeping with your husband.

This is the only part of her life that can't be examined, admired, or discussed out loud. It's the only part of her life she doesn't respect herself for, and it keeps her miserable even when she's happy.

She knows that whatever happiness she has is stolen: shoplifted and illegitimate. She's not a fool, even though she knows she's acting like one.

Or she's not sleeping with your husband. Maybe you're single; maybe you have different relationships in your life—and so this is a friend of yours, a woman you've consider a dependable part of your life. She's an elementary school teacher, a physical therapist, a bank executive, an engineer, a computer programmer. She's been your friend since junior high, your colleague, your neighbor, your confidante, without revealing this part of her life to you, because she suspects that even at your most understanding, you wouldn't understand.

You couldn't unless you've been through this, and she knows you haven't. Or she thinks she knows you haven't. But one thing she has learned is that nobody is exempt from the possibility of this happening—if a person could claim exemption, she'd be first on the list.

So she doesn't tell you, her best friend. You might judge her harshly or, even worse, stop speaking to her altogether, and she can't bear the thought of losing you. She's already surrounded by the possibility of loss and will not add to it even at the cost of not talking about the very thing that consumes her waking moments.

Educated, polite, and brought up by a loving family, she's not a particularly hot tomato or the kind of woman usually transported across state lines for immoral purposes. Kind, attentive, and considerate, she is deeply committed to those she loves, and that's one of the reasons this tears her apart. One of the things she loves about this man, after all, is the way he treats the ones to whom he is closest.

Not her—he can't treat her as if she were really in his life, after all—but others. His real family, the inhabitants of his real life. If he were an emotional bully or an emotional slob, she wouldn't have been drawn to him. She understands how divided he is, how he feels like a piece of meat being sliced up by a rusty knife, how he feels like he's drowning and suffocating and being eaten alive all at once. He, too, is a decent person, except for this business of loving someone he isn't meant to love.

Holidays are hard, but so is spring; so are winter nights, summer mornings, and long early-autumn afternoons. The phone is her lifeline, and she has about seventeen different ways of being reached. She'll take what she can get—not a way anyone would think of her, but in this case it's true. There are codes they use to communicate what can't be spoken or written; these were funny at first, but over time they have become as serious as a car crash.

Maybe it ends when there *is* a car crash, and they're in the front seat together, returning from a place they never should have been, suddenly having to make up a series of lies to disguise what everybody around them realizes is the truth. Even if they get away with it, the experience wrecks them, mangles what they had beyond recognition. Or she goes to his kid's high school graduation and realizes that it's been twelve years already and that she could have had a kid herself by now, one in the sixth grade.

Or it continues. Impossible nights, intolerable weekends, endless violations of her essential self. Yet they have loved each other for so long now, how can it stop? She starts to worry that he'll die of a heart attack and no one will tell her. Or she wonders about her own final moments. This is the worst.

She can't believe this is her life. Nobody else would believe it either, even the man. It's a tough, rotten, exhausting routine. Nobody chooses it on purpose. This is not a defense of her. She knows better than you that what she's doing is indefensible. Don't ridicule her, and don't think you don't know her. You do.

That Girl

by JIANNA HEUER

Let me just begin by saying I am complicit. I watched The Girl fall, twist, and break, and I, like everyone else, did nothing to stop it.

It was the first day of high school for her, the last year of high school for me. I watched the four sophomores. They stalked The Girl like prey. She wore too much makeup, had long beautiful hair and a brand-new dress. They could smell her insecurity and eagerness to be accepted; she would be easy pickings.

They pounced while she was alone. The group of sophomore girls made a circle around her. She was paralyzed as they started.

"You think you're hot shit, huh?"

"Slut."

"Whore."

"Did you wear that to get all the attention you could?"

"You are such a skank. I'm going to make your time here miserable."

Each one took turns attacking her. It was brutal to watch.

What a terrible start for The Girl. The sophomores were not bluffing. They would throw things at her, start rumors, call her names, and ostracize her. They would grow more malicious when she started dating their friend. The Girl had swum in their pool. Now they were going to drown her. These attacks, these rumors, these assignations—these other girls would change her life irrevocably.

On the day they started tormenting her, she was a virgin. She had yet to kiss a boy. The instant she was labeled "slut," something changed. It didn't happen right away. It took time for the rumors to mold her and for the constant harassment to take effect.

As her freshman year came to an end, the vice-principal pulled her aside before homeroom.

"Your shirt is not compliant with the dress code."

"The shirt I'm wearing now?" The Girl challenged.

"Yes. I will have to write you up."

The Girl searched the halls for her friend with the A cup. They had laughed that morning because they had worn the same shirt to school. She saw her a few lockers away and pointed.

"Is her shirt in violation?" The Girl asked.

"No, that shirt's fine," the vice-principle replied slowly.

"It's the same shirt."

"No, I don't think it is. It can't be . . ."

"Would you like to look at both tags?"

As I witnessed the encounter, I saw the vice-principal look down at The Girl and smirk. She said, "People with certain body types just can't wear this type of shirt. On your body, it is not in compliance with the dress code. You have cleavage." There was no rule about cleavage. This was administration reinforcing what the sophomore girls started. School-sanctioned body-shaming.

The Girl did make friends despite that low hum, that background noise of people talking about what she did, who she did. Building friendships under these conditions was difficult. They lacked stability and were fragile. It's hard to believe that people care for you when you are one of the most hated people in the school.

That first boyfriend lasted until the summer before sophomore year. He cheated with her best friend while The Girl was away on a family trip. Her best friend was the main link to the group of friends she had. She severed those ties and was adrift in an unstable world. She started to see the rumors as something she could rely on, a constant.

When you are young you are malleable. The sophomores gave the girl an identity. She was notorious, but being known for something, even this, is better than not existing, right?

I watched, as so many of us did, as she become "That Girl." She claimed "Slut." She owned it and merged with it. It was her protection. If she said it first, it would hurt less when she overheard the others talk about her.

Despite that, she, like so many others, was shoved, pushed, and she staggered as she sunk into that role. As we watched, we became part of the reason she fell.

She got quieter, smaller, failed classes, and came to school less. She was lost both within herself and to anyone who wanted to know her.

She barely graduated. She left this time of her life hoping for something better but lacking the belief it existed. Her trust was broken and the ability to be close to anyone taken—not by the boys she had let use her body, but by the girls who had taken her dignity.

Stability

by HEIDI ROCKEFELLER

I learned early on that it was not okay for me to talk openly about being treated for mental illness. If I'm guarded in my approach when sharing my story, it's out of a sense of self-preservation.

A little background might help:

When I was eighteen, I was in a head-on car accident that happened as I was heading home one evening after working on a final project during my freshman year at a local university. Approximately two months after that accident, I lost touch with reality, had a nervous breakdown, and was diagnosed with paranoid schizophrenia.

As the years passed, my parents were urged to tell extended family of my condition. When they related the news to Aunt Tressa, she suggested they look into the possibility of a traumatic brain injury. As it turned out, Aunt Tressa was right. I had a closed brain injury that had been missed the night of the accident. I was facing two problems: It had been more than two years since the initial injury, and for most of those years I had been very heavily medicated. When the doctors tried to wean me off the medications, I fell back into a pattern of agitation and insomnia.

That car accident was more than thirty years ago now, and I have discovered that I cannot survive without daily medication. Having been re-diagnosed as bipolar (whether or not that diagnosis is exactly right), I know the medication helps me live a relatively ordinary life.

At times I considered the side effects and experimented with a few days off the meds, just to see what would happen. Everything would speed up; I would get more anxious and need less sleep. Then, after days of this, I would need no sleep at all. For a little while it might feel good—until it didn't.

Then the edges would fray.

My husband would be increasingly anxious, because he knew my pattern. After a manic episode, a depressive one would inevitably follow and last for a few weeks. Those were brutal.

When my two daughters were very young, I devised a plan with my husband to help me stay on my medication. It became his job to hand me my pills every night before bed, because somehow it was easier to take them if they came from the hand of someone who loved me. We came up with that routine on our own. It didn't always feel right or safe to bring other people in.

My husband and I have been faithful members of our church community for years, but somehow it didn't feel as though church was the place to gather support for mental health and wellness. The prayer chain is riddled with requests for people with all sorts of difficulties, but you will never see a request from a young mother so deep in a depressive episode that she fantasizes daily about ending her pain. When I did open up at church, sometimes I heard things like "You don't need medication. God will heal you." This is a sweet sentiment, but the worst temptation for someone like me.

Once, I was picking up my prescriptions from the pharmacy when the tech came out from behind the counter. In a conspiratorial tone she told me, "You don't really need these. You should come to this thing we're having at my church." She crossed a line. She had no idea of the dangerous game she was playing. She had my life in her hands but, in a strange twist of fate, she put her job in mine.

Two things occur to me. When I tell someone that I am being treated for mental illness and they respond with "You don't need that medication," they are judging me in my fully medicated state. And there are very few people who have witnessed the symptoms I am keeping at bay with the help of daily medication. There is a misconception with mental illness that needs to be left behind. I do not take these pills because I am weak, or because I am occasionally sad. I take them because without them I will die. I hope the day will come when people will not tell other people, based on little to no information, that they do not need their medications. Until that day comes, I will continue to tell my story in the hopes that it can help someone with a similar tale.

Good Girls

by ILENE BECKERMAN

I was a "good girl" in high school. Being a virgin was a virtue if you were a teenage girl in the 1950s. To "lose it" was a tragedy. Growing up, we were told stories about the birds and the bees, the stork, and even about fields of cabbage patches, but I never could figure out what went where.

When Joanie (I'm not using her last name in case her grandchildren read this) eventually confessed junior year in high school that she had "done it," nobody wanted to be her friend anymore. We thought her fallen state might be catching.

The movies were no help. Mothers and fathers as portrayed in the movies had to sleep in twin beds. If a husband wanted to kiss his wife goodnight and she was in bed, he had to keep one foot on the floor. If we thought something was "going to happen," the movie screen jumped to a fire blazing in a fireplace.

Even if a boy pleaded and said he loved me, I still couldn't do it because of my underwear. There was too much of it. "Those parts" of a girl's body were covered up and not allowed to move.

A bra had dangerous points. If a boy got too close to the points, he'd be stabbed. Not by a safety pin or the girl herself, but by the unyielding fabric of the cone-shaped brassiere. Some girls couldn't fill out the points, so they'd stuff their bra with Kleenex.

I only needed Kleenex when I had a cold.

Even if you had a body like Audrey Hepburn, you'd still have to wear a girdle. I remember being imprisoned in an incredibly uncomfortable virginity-protector girdle. It came with four long dangling garters for your stockings. A "good girl" never went out with bare legs unless she was wearing bobby socks. I always wore stockings on a date and wore heels unless my date (heaven forbid) was shorter than me.

The underpants. More Victorian than Victoria's Secret.

Over your underpants you wore a slip. It only came in virginal white, because what else would it be?

The crinoline. At least one, possibly two, so your skirt would stick out and you wouldn't. And then your clothes. By the time a sixteen-year-old boy tried to undo all your body armor, his passion had already exploded.

If you had your period (frequently called "the curse"), you also had to wear a sanitary belt and a Kotex or Modess sanitary napkin.

I wore all that on a "date." Having a date for Saturday night was the most important thing if you grew up in Manhattan like I did. Maybe teens who lived in faraway places like the Bronx were different.

Most dates, I double-dated with my best friend, Dora. Dora always got the good guys. I got her leftovers.

I never went on a date to the malt shop with a boy, as girls did in the movies. In Manhattan, everybody lived in apartment buildings. No backyards, no cars, and no malt shops. The only place to make out was in the balcony of a movie theater, which had an extra benefit—you could smoke. I saw a lot of movies, but I really didn't see them, because I wouldn't wear my glasses on a date.

Dora always fixed me up with rich boys from preppy schools. We went to fancy clubs at swanky hotels. They never proofed us, because we looked older. The bands played the foxtrot; my dates danced too close and apparently thought that if they blew in my ear, it would feel romantic.

Who gave them such terrible advice?

Even worse, we had to order a drink. I always ordered a brandy Alexander. It almost tasted like a malted. The best part of those dates was collecting cocktail stirrers.

Dora and I made up a code for things we did and didn't do. I shall now reveal the code:

One was kissing.
Two was necking.
Three was petting above the waist.
Four was petting below the waist.
Five was going all the way.
Dora and I only did one and two.
We had no equivalent numbers for boys. We never considered going anywhere on them.
The truth is, we never wanted to do "it."
We just wanted to have a boyfriend and be madly in love.
Eventually, I learned what went where—and had six children.
That's what being "Good" got you.

Leveling the Playing Field

by JUDGE ROSIE SPEEDLIN GONZALEZ

My mother, Alicia, was driven. She always had big dreams for both my brother and me. Both she and my father believed that a good education would level any playing field, and that it would pay out when it came to our quality of life.

For her the path to success was straight and narrow: She believed there was one clear, delineated, single road leading to specific and universally desirable destination. There was, for example, that afternoon when my mom came to pick me up from basketball practice when I was in junior high. Mr. Solis, a kind custodian, decided to give her a "compliment" and told her, in a charming voice, that I would make a great coach one day. He imagined he was offering high praise. My mother "set him straight" without hesitation, however, announcing to Mr. Solis that coaching would not become my line of work.

I would become either a doctor or a lawyer, she said. No other options were offered. Plus, she only paid for "A" grades: Literally, she gave me and my brother a dollar if we earned an A, raising the amount to $10 by the time we were in high school. Being good in school, it seemed, paid off early.

I chose a small New England school in Vermont, where I studied Liberal Arts and Government, until the second Vermont winter took a heavy toll. I returned to Texas and received my BA in Political Science from St. Mary's University in San Antonio.

Afterward, I *should* have disciplined myself to study for, and actually take, the LSAT. Instead, I focused on the "ME" culture of the mid-1980s, with a minor in nightclubs and debauchery.

An advisor nudged me into a master's in Public Administration, and although the rest should have been history, I began floundering again. Distracted and without direction, I dropped out. This marked the beginning of a decade of working in social services. I did everything from investigating child abuse, gang cases, and teens dabbling with drug use; I taught students with special needs.

Then my father became ill, and my mother asked that I move back home to help her.

There I was, back at home in my late twenties. It felt like a fall backward until I rediscovered the mother who urged me to revisit the dream of law school she held for me. Personally, I'd left that dream behind somewhere between Vermont and a club in the '80s, but now I actually studied for the LSAT. I took a prep course.

I returned to St. Mary's, but this time for Law, as a nontraditional student.

Achieving a law degree did not make everything easy, however. The cutthroat culture of law wasn't necessarily prepared for someone like me—perhaps because of my age or LGBTQIA status. But that didn't stop me from zealously representing the disenfranchised, the formerly incarcerated, and members of otherwise marginalized communities, including women and children. My title might have changed, but the core components of my vocation had not: I was a formidable advocate for those who needed a powerful voice.

Now, when I can step back from the gavel and the bench, I see that I've become in several respects a kind of "coach," despite my mother's warning. Yes, I am in a courtroom and in law offices, operating in arenas different from the basketball court as I preside as a judge, but I have spent my life encouraging others to show up and perform better. I did it as a case manager, as a probation officer, as their lawyer, and now as the judge that presides over their family violence cases.

The journey of my life—Texas to Vermont and back—brought me to where I stand today: wiser, more experienced, time-tested, and supportive of those in need. If you want to perform better and I can help, I'm ready. If the lessons I learned in navigating my circuitous journey can help you map yours, I'm here. My legacy, as I see it, is to leave the world a better and fairer place than we found it, through verdicts of encouragement, justice, and love.

While we've often disagreed, my mother and I, I believe that she would share this perspective. We are born into this world with our skills to perform, and to perform them well. If we're lucky, maybe we encounter the right person, pass all the signposts from I-35/US 281, and eventually reach the place where we embrace humanity, generosity, compassion, and kindness.

Rubbers

by KATHERINE JIMENEZ

When I was eight years old, we slept in a low-grade, overpriced Miami room, having moved from Nicaragua three years earlier. Our small apartment had thin walls and mold growing on the bathroom ceiling, just too high up for my too-short mother to clean. It was a time when the three of us—mom, son, daughter—shared the same bed. It was all my mother's job at a Cuban restaurant could afford.

I remember it as a year with holes, like a damaged film negative, a flame burning passed the edges to where a sharp picture once was. I try to find the colors of that year in my mind but can only see black and white, a filter clouding memories of an empty fridge and empty stomachs. My mother, however, remains a flashbulb in every picture of my childhood, from the moments she leaned cleaning over a tub to the sweat stains on her white busboy shirt.

That year my mother and thirteen-year-old brother sat on the living room couch. I remained in the bedroom flipping through TV channels until I got bored and peered from below the slit of the open door separating the gray walls. The two of them were facing each other, hunching over something red in my mother's hands. It sounded plastic, almost rubber, as she inserted the open end over two of her fingers. *A balloon*, I thought. I opened the door wider to reveal myself.

"I want one! I want one!" I shouted, but my mother only laughed and shook her head. "Why?" I felt my anger rising.

"It's not a balloon," she replied.

I asked her what it was, and when she didn't answer, I called her a liar. She scolded me back to the bedroom, told me to not eavesdrop like those women who left dents on plastic window blinds. I cried into

47

my pillow, only learning years later that balloons came in more than one color. Years when I realized that mothers excused their sons and shamed their daughters. Years when I taught myself to keep my own secrets the way my mother kept hers.

Even after the first boy, first kiss, first one, even after I got my period and grew out my breasts, my mother never showed me that balloon. I was waiting for the moment she'd talk to me the way she talked to my brother. When she would tell me about the messy, awkward, unknown realities of the adult world that were supposed to be so foreign to my innocent imagination because I had made the mistake of being born a girl.

Cover your eyes. Don't look at that, she used to say when the tele-novela sex scenes came on. But my brother was still allowed to watch the heroine spread her legs. He had a privilege I never did. He could call women "whores," even talk about strip clubs and prostitutes. He could tell her about the women he had been with and the ones he was still waiting for. He remained her son. In my mother's eyes, I remained an illusion of someone I no longer was. I knew this when I asked her about my own balloon years later, except mine was in the shape of a pill.

"I just think it's important to be prepared," I insisted.

"For what? You don't have a husband. You don't need that." She scrutinized my face. "Have you done those things?"

But I wouldn't let myself break under her disapproving gaze. I lied. She still cried. I felt dirty, as if I had betrayed all her years of hard work, that her hands had turned rough for nothing.

What sin had I committed that my brother hadn't? Were we so different in biology that to look at me was to look at a different crea-ture entirely? We could not be judged on the same scale. Otherwise, I wouldn't have wanted to peel off the fingertips that someone else had left on my skin. He could be touched and not disintegrate under our mother's expectations.

48

I know what she convinces herself I am. I'm old enough now to understand she likes to play pretend. We sit in our new living room with an ultra-HD television, watching all the scenes I couldn't witness as a child. She plays her game of ignorance—where only half of me is spared for the sake of her comfort, while the other is left to wither to my own silence.

Uncharted

by EMILY HEIDEN

My life had gone according to plan. I was twenty-nine and beginning my second master's degree, attending graduate school for creative writing in Washington DC.

In the first week of the program, I was invited to a poetry reading. I wore a navy dress and red lipstick, which went well with my blonde hair.

One of the men who got up to the mic that night read a poem so electric it set a spark in me to thrumming. It also didn't hurt that he had beautiful dark hair; a straight, perfect nose; and a hungry, ready look.

A friend told me his name was Mason. I found him online, messaged him, and complimented his poem. He wrote back and asked to see my work. Soon after that, we were flirting at every event.

It didn't take long until we were sleeping together. It often took him days to call afterward, which only made me more of a goner. His silence confirmed a belief I had about myself: I wasn't good enough to love. We started having sex each week after class. A month in, I started the pill, and this faint whiff of a future—even just a sexual one—scared him off. He ended things with me.

I went home and stared at the yellow plastic pill pack, then flushed its contents in anger. But a month later, motivated by lust and wounded pride, I called my doctor and refilled my prescription in an if-you-build-it, he-will-come endeavor. I would find a way to get him back.

Around this time, a new friend in the program, Savannah, asked me what birth control method I used. When I told her, she replied, "Why put synthetic hormones into your body? You should try charting." She showed me a binder full of grid-lined paper and talked about how well this method worked for her. Eventually she persuaded me. Why *did*

I want to put synthetic hormones in my body, if all it took to prevent pregnancy was learning more about my cycle?

I stopped taking the pill again and instead started charting my cycle.

And I completely ignored Mason. Every Wednesday in class, I talked to each man but him. It took two months for this to work, but eventually he cracked.

One night, I told myself before sleeping with him that I was on day 8 of my cycle, and it was therefore not possible to get pregnant.

Two weeks later, two blue lines blinked up at me from a plastic wand.

This was not a part of the plan.

I agonized about my situation for a month, talked to every friend who would listen, and at six weeks along, took a train to Manhattan and had an abortion.

After, I was shattered. I felt like I should have been educated enough not to fall for some hippie method.

It didn't help that other women judged me. My roommate told her friend Melissa what happened to me, and Melissa replied, "Oof. Not that many women have abortions."

I did some reading and discovered that Melissa was wrong. In 2013, the year I got pregnant, one in three women in America would have an abortion. Today it's one in four, but abortion is still incredibly common. It just isn't talked about openly. Powerful stigma surrounds this experience.

Five years later, a friend asked if I wanted to become an abortion doula, which is an emotional support person. I was nervous but completed the training, and soon I had my first shift at Planned Parenthood.

On that day, I watched woman after woman walk through the procedure room doors. I was astonished at how many people I saw, and how different they were. There were twentysomethings in Lululemon yoga pants. Thirtysomethings with nose rings and purple hair. Soccer moms talking about their kid's upcoming game.

Seeing them, a new understanding swept through me. I had not fallen from grace, and neither had they. We had all simply gotten pregnant and decided to have an abortion. It was not necessary to attach a shameful narrative to it. I did so because when something is left to the shadows, we think it unique to us, and thus morph common events into matters of personal failure. I decided to do what I could to help each of my doula patients from descending into this line of thinking, like I had. "I've had one too," I told them, gripping their hands. "You are not alone."

Feminism and Mom

by ANNE BAGAMERY

"It will be so nice when you don't have to do this anymore."

With just a few words, uttered twenty years ago, my mother blasted apart my lifelong image of her as a feminist—and showed me that, deep down, I had failed her.

I was visiting for a few weeks with my daughter, who was about ten. After long days of swimming, shopping, and sightseeing, I'd tuck my daughter into bed and my mother and I would sit up late, watching TV and catching up.

Mom was a woman of her time: smart, ambitious, and stifled. Raised during the Depression and World War II, she was both a varsity cheerleader and valedictorian of her high school class. She entered college hoping to study bacteriology but wound up majoring in Home Economics, which her parents felt was a more appropriate field for a woman.

She met my father in college and worked a bit after they were married, but stopped when his career took off and my brother and I were born. For twelve years, as Dad moved up the corporate ladder, Mom was literally a homemaker, settling us every two years into new schools and bigger houses, finding her place with volunteer work and the entertainment expected of a corporate wife.

Then the marriage fell apart. It was rancorous, and Dad was not generous. We had just moved into a house that needed work, and my brother and I had just started at private school. Alimony would cover either the house or our schooling, not both.

Mom mobilized. She negotiated financial aid and set out to find a job. But with twenty years off the market, she basically had to start over.

Her first job was in the kitchen of a church—organizing lunches, dinners, and teas, sometimes for two hundred people, often seven days a week. It was backbreaking work, but we got leftovers.

To keep her mind alive, Mom volunteered at the local hospital. Soon her unit offered her a full-time job. Then a bigger unit offered her a job running it. By the time she retired, she had fifty people reporting to her, from typists to doctors.

Years later, when my own marriage was foundering and I needed to mobilize, Mom was my role model. As I navigated a job search, divorce, and then balancing career and child, she was my cheerleader: "You can do it!"

That summer, though, when I complained about my job—as one does—Mom didn't soothe or sympathize. She sighed:

"It will be so nice when you don't have to do this anymore."

"Do what, exactly?"

"Work! When you get married again and can give up your job!"

What?

"But . . . but . . . ," I sputtered. "I love to work! Even if I remarried, I'd still work! I mean, didn't you love your work?"

Another sigh. "I regarded work as something I had to do—that I was forced to do."

More sputtering "But . . . but . . . I thought that going back to work was your finest hour! You built a career out of nothing! And you kept us afloat!"

More sighing. "The happiest moments of my life were when your dad was a young executive, and I kept our house and raised you kids. The rest . . . I could have skipped.

"And," she added, "that was the life I wanted for you."

I was gobsmacked. How could she not know me better? How could I have totally misunderstood her?

But here's the thing: I didn't start a conversation. I didn't present my point of view or ask her about hers. I just shut down. And things were never quite the same between us.

Did I fail my mother? Oh, sure. Not by openly disobeying her or refusing to do what she wanted me to do, but by a far more hurtful transgression: rejecting her dream.

Did my mother fail me? Here, I'm not so sure. I could have opened up to her more about what I wanted from life, and why. I just assumed that she would see—and in seeing, understand.

Maybe it's like what they say about the cobbler's children who have no shoes. My career has been in communication, and here, when it really counted, I spectacularly failed to do just that.

That's a mistake I hope I won't make again.

Rituals

by NICOLE CATARINO

At fourteen, I stop believing in God and create a church.

I write hymns to mumble into pillows at odd minutes. I hoard rocks from the road for rosaries. I build pews from the foam of my childhood bed and hold my head for baptism under the shower. My jagged fingernails *tap tap tap* coded prayers onto the parts of my body I've deemed holy. My small knuckles, washed constantly, flush red with penance. I take the world's salvation into my small piano hands. I become my most loyal disciple.

Inside my cathedral walls, I plead for sanctuary. Bells ring in the echoes of silence as I, alone at the altar, eyes pinched shut, chant under my breath: *Please don't let anything bad happen to my friends and family. Please don't let anything bad happen to me.*

By the time I turn eighteen, the responses are instinctive: Five servings, take four; food touched is food declined; hands held out in invitation are left to dangle. Stomach growls, dry tongues, and a lingering appetite are my remains. This is what life will always be: starving, and letting myself go hungry.

At a friend's nineteenth-birthday party, a girl I'll never know— tripping over her own quick-stuttered feet, incited by too many shots of cheap strawberry Svedka—stumbles into the bleach-white dorm bathroom. I, as always, am sober. I, as always, am washing my hands. She falls into the stall closest to the door, ignoring me where I stiffened with dawning dread against the sink, favoring her more pressing concern over my stifled gasp.

I remember nothing but the throbbing of my heartbeat in my skull; the water, too much soap; the flight or fight turned tail as paralysis finally gave way to the solo thought of *GET OUT!* I shoulder the door with all my weight and move on legs that aren't mine.

My hands are shaking. I shove them into my pockets. I fall into an open chair in the birthday girl's room before my knees give out, and plaster on feigned exhaustion.

Two friends are leaving, walking around the room giving out goodbye hugs like communion. When one turns toward me, I give her a grin and fall into her arms, minding my hands, minding my tremors. I move to pull back from the embrace, and she doesn't let go.

I take my hands off the small of her back, say her name once, softly, and she doesn't let go. My shoulders start to shake. She doesn't let go.

In her arms, I thaw into sobs. I have never been hugged for this long in my life, and for twenty long minutes of weeping and hushed humming, she doesn't let me go.

(March 2020)

In my childhood home, I've become what my mother calls a "nervous wreck." What I've really become is a creature of ugly habits. Someone who lets their hands crack like pottery for the sake of making sure everything around me smells like disinfectant. I wash them too often and don't apply enough lotion, my doctor says. She tells me it's normal, given the circumstances. I wonder if she missed the spots of dried blood along my fate lines.

Affection become an afterthought. Why would I *want* anyone to touch me? Why would I *want* anyone to love me?

(What do I do when I want nothing more than to throw myself out the door and fall into the arms of the first person who will hold me? Hold *me*, like that's all they've ever been born to do, and their kindness alone is enough to stave away whatever crawls on their palms?)

It's easier to be angry at what I don't have than to want it. I know how to bare teeth, spit with rage, twitch a mouth into a permanent scowl. I know how to keep *away*. If I live like this, I can sleep knowing one truth:

No one will ever touch me again.

At twenty-one, the nurse takes to asking if I'm a virgin with all the surprise of someone who expected better. She wants me to correct her, tell her a story: *"There was this one boy . . ."* or *"Not counting the girl the summer before . . ."* I offer no relief. I shrug, tell her yes, pick at the skin around my nails.

I remember the feeling of another hand in mine, because I hold my own to sleep. I want to tell her this. Where would she write it on my chart?

Hysterectomy Hysteria

by MICHELLE P. CARTER

If you had the misfortune of being born with a uterus—and also of being born in America—then you've probably had the displeasure of experiencing the dumpster fire that is the United States health-care system. You want an abortion? Drive across state lines, and that'll be $1,000. A hysterectomy? You have to have three kids already and your husband's permission, and that'll be $26,000. Birth control? Don't know her. You're a trans man looking for gender-affirming surgery? Call me when you've done a thorough psych eval—and the answer will still be no.

Going to a doctor in America when you possess a uterus is like falling into a crater of shit, and then being expected to claw your way out while an amorphous behemoth squats over the opening like a giant toilet, asking, "Have you tried just losing weight?"

I don't want kids; I never did. And my periods have been excruciating for more than twenty years. Like crawling-on-the-floor-at-my-office-to-get-to-the-medicine-cabinet excruciating. I've known since I was still posting emo songs on Myspace that I wanted to get a hysterectomy. But I also knew that path was littered with medical gaslighting, procreation propaganda, and anti-feminist rhetoric—all of which, of course, I would have to contend with in my aforementioned crater of shit.

Almost as if I knew our garbage Supreme Court was going to overturn *Roe v. Wade* mere months later, I began exploring getting a hysterectomy in February of 2022. I hadn't seen an OB-GYN in more than six years because the last person to give me a pap smear was crowned "Most Likely to Yell at a Crying Patient until Her Cervix Clamps Shut" in high school.

I had no idea what to expect. What I definitely *didn't* expect was to meet my new OB-GYN and walk out eleven minutes later with the promise of a hysterectomy.

She didn't even perform a pelvic exam. She just listened (and looked at my medical history). Then she said, "I'm going to put in a request for your surgery." I was outside of my body—much like my uterus would be soon. I couldn't believe it. I *didn't* believe it. A doctor who listens? To a woman? Couldn't be.

I left the hospital a hysterical mess, crying and snotting into my face mask. I filmed a blubbering TikTok about it in my car, as you do. I called my husband, who was perplexed by my sobbing. "Okay . . . Um . . . Isn't that what you wanted?" he asked. "YEAH, I THOUGHT YOU WOULD BE HAPPIER ABOUT THIS!" I screamed, circling the parking garage levels. "Oh! Oh, I am! Oh, you're HAPPY!" he exclaimed as I snot-cried into my AirPods.

Doc said surgery could take three months minimum to get scheduled. "Wow, that's sooner than I thought!" I mused. Because, of course, I expected to wade through the shit for at least nine months. Then I got a call two weeks later to schedule it for March 10th. "Of this year?" I asked. Yes; as in . . . *three weeks from then.*

I was no longer falling into a crater of shit. I was floating out of it.

The surgery was . . . remarkably unremarkable? One minute I was cracking jokes with the anesthesiologist, the next a nurse was waking me and asking, "How are you feeling?" In my drugged-up comedown, I said, "Well, it hurts less than any of my periods, so I guess I made the right choice."

My mother flew across the country to be my live-in nurse for the week of my recovery. Turns out, that wasn't even necessary. Ten minutes after I walked in the door, I was in the kitchen making chicken quesadillas. After three days, I was pain-free and pooping again. I'm still not entirely convinced they actually took anything out, except for the fact that I stopped menstruating and I'm a lot nicer to my husband.

I marvel every day at the privilege and fortune I had to get my hysterectomy. But so many uterus-people are still wading through that shit crater without any hope of getting out of it, except to fall into debt or an early grave. Everyone deserves access to the health care they need—not just White folks who won the insurance lottery.

It's more important than ever for us to fight for each other so that my story isn't so inexplicably atypical. If our doctors won't advocate for us, then we will.

Too many have fallen before us; it's time to break the cycle.

I Can Keep a Secret

by LOUISA BALLHAUS

I meet Courtney at work in June, and right away I know I'm in trouble. She has bleached-blonde hair and a raspy voice and stands half a foot shorter than I do. She can't weigh more than ninety-eight pounds. At least once a week, she comes back to the office with a mountain of Taco Bell. She tells me she vaped outside on her break, and this, to me, is the most daring, badass thing I've ever heard.

Courtney has tattoos up and down her arms, and she's impressed with me by the end of my first day. Later that week, she tells me she was thinking: *Okay, this girl can actually answer phones!* A relief. More time for her to flirt with film executives in the hallways, more time to make jokes and get high at lunch. Courtney and I work in Client Services, but I'm grateful to hide behind the telephone these first few weeks. I can't yet offer what she does. Naomi, older and even more glamorous, coos over my rings, the Armani skirt I no longer fit into.

"A lot of the time, it's just about making things nice to look at," Naomi explains of our roles at the office. It's clear she isn't just talking about the furniture.

By the middle of summer, I am desperate. Courtney and I are tasked with setting up the bar for an end-of-week happy hour, and I stand on a chair while she points out the liquor and glasses we'll need from the top shelf. When I hand them over, I could swear she had flicked her eyes away just a second sooner, like she didn't want me to see what she was looking at. I'm still on the clock for another few hours, but she offers me a drink if I promise not to tell. I'm pretty sure she's my boss (who would I tell?), but I agree.

I can keep a secret.

She pours our drinks, and I learn about her life. Courtney, unlike me, has real aspirations in film, not just a family member with a good connection. She has a few projects under her belt and big ideas about what she'd do if she got the chance. *It's why she's so invested in forming relationships at the office*, I tell myself often, marveling at how she lights up in conversation hour after hour.

It's why she's invested in forming a relationship with you, a cold part of my mind replies.

I have stopped listening to her, I realize, too taken with how she looks mixing drinks behind the bar. But she's said something important: "This girl I used to date was there." Something flickers in my chest. Within the hour, I've worked a mention of my high school girlfriend into the conversation. I watch her doggedly for a reaction.

By August, I've been to Courtney's apartment on the Lower East Side a handful of times and learned that she sells Ecstasy to help pay her bills and take care of her black cat, Mystery. She has a bedroom that could have been in a '90s teen movie, one wall completely consumed by magazine clippings, photos, and a giant poster of Britney Spears over the bed. We smoke weed and watch TV, and I watch her sell drugs, marveling here just like I do at the office.

I'm going back to school in the fall, and we still haven't kissed by the end of summer. I tell myself we work together and maybe that's it, but I watch her pass out lit joints and key bumps at office parties and am reminded that the usual rules don't apply. Why can't I kiss her?

Courtney's not afraid of anything, but sometimes when our fingers touch, I feel like she's holding her breath. I step outside the latest happy hour and light a cigarette, wondering if it's about me or about everyone else: how they might respond to this even despite all the other lines she's crossed. I know how people can be, how quickly they can turn on you.

It starts to rain. I think of all the things Courtney doesn't try to hide, what people have asked me to show and to put away over the years. Eventually, she comes looking for me and laughs at me for standing outside and getting wet. We don't kiss until December, when I sleep over under her Britney Spears poster. It feels like we've both been waiting a long time.

Gingerbread Woman

by CLAIRE LASHER

We were made by a world that wants to take a bite out of us, curated by hungry eyes and dripping mouths. Inhuman appetites and blunt teeth just waiting to dig in. The traditional recipe for an American Girl must be followed meticulously: sugar, spice, and shame. Society cuts girls into the right shape like blunt metal, pressing soft flesh into rigid molds—not too fat, not too skinny.

I spent years yearning to be palatable, to entice everyone who met me. To be uninviting was to be impolite; to be undesirable was to be defective. My value was calculated based on my ability to nourish others. I found myself offering up pieces of myself in order to satiate someone else's appetite. Yet each bite taken out left me a little more hollow. Carved out around the ribs.

I've come to understand that life is worth more than the flattery that comes from people wanting to consume you. My best qualities are not crowd-pleasers. Bitter turmeric, burning chili, or acidic lemon seed oil turn some tongues away. Freedom is found in understanding that deterring the wayward appetites of strangers is a luxury, not a loss.

Life before this realization is akin to sitting in an oven. The heat is slow and constant. One day you wake up with wide eyes and look past the glass walls that house you, catching sight of giants wandering past and looking down, wondering *Are they done? Can I touch? Can I take a bite? CanIbiteCanIbiteCanIBite?* On that day, I did what any reasonable creature would.

I *ran.*

I want this moment for every young girl almost as much as I mourn it. Life outside the oven isn't the safe haven it seems from inside. No matter how far you run, there are always new teeth nipping at your heels. It is a lonelier experience than you would expect, given the number of women running it at a time.

My mother has lived her life unapologetically. Usually we run together, but she has her own battle scars and bite marks. She remains unbothered, baffled at the urgency with which I avoid gaining my own. She reminds me that scars are signs of life, that a pristine existence is rarely an exciting one.

In running away, I left my bra behind, and I've never felt better. Our bodies are unprofessional. Even our outline under layers of fabric is a distraction to others. They'll resent you for your brash acceptance (men and women both; men for tempting their appetite and women for triggering the shame baked into their own skin).

People want to cover you unless they're selling you, or selling to you. Run *faster*.

There are men who have failed to recognize that I might be arsenic laced. Wandering mouths and hands. *"It is in your nature to be bitten into, you bitch."* They sit impatiently at the table, having only ever been instructed to consume. These are the men you run *over*.

So we run. We all run, and run, and run. We dodge sticky fingers and honey tongues until we are breathless. The thing about this race is that it aches. It is not a game. There is not a prize at the end. The goal is to reach a finish line, one we limp across unknowingly at different parts of our lives because it's never been defined.

Inevitably, there will be bite marks and bruises. But there are ways to fill those spaces. Spun sugar, some optimism, a blind eye to the fact that it doesn't all fit together quite right. The end result is something you've made for yourself; you are not less whole because of it. The end of your story does not take place in the bottom of someone else's stomach. It ends with sugar-spun women with turmeric, garlic, saffron, and salt.

The only person she's been built to nourish is herself.

Baba's Mirror

by PIA L. BERTUCCI

In a university course I once taught on women writers, I presented a list of labels to my students for discussion—*slut, whore, frump, spinster*—words that have traditionally classified women according to their sexual activity, or lack thereof. However, to quote the modern hero Hermione Granger: "Fear of the name" only perpetuates that stigma.

Far more insidious are unspoken assessments of women's virtue. Names can be repeated until they cease to have meaning, but tacit judgments are impenetrable.

Growing up in Chicago in the '70s and '80s, I found this silent code to be prevalent among many immigrant cultures. My grandparents—Italian on one side, Czech on the other—with their refined use of language devoid of vulgarities, were no exception.

Both sides were working class who cherished family and tradition. They celebrated their respective heritages through their cuisine, whether it was lasagna or *Svíčková*. They were also fervent Catholics, the pre-Vatican II-reform kind that fasted during Lent, ate fish on Friday, and instilled guilt in subsequent generations.

My Italian grandparents ran a mom-and-pop near St. Simon's and Central Steel. Workers zipped in for a sandwich or a 25-cent jumbo pickle; kids bought candy; the so-called "Sainted Sisters" picked up sweet rolls after church; and more than a few regulars, after doing their shopping, lingered at the counter to gossip with my grandma.

After school, when I wasn't roller-skating the back alleys, I would hide out between the gumball machines and Anna-Banana pop. I'd overhear discussions of "the other woman," the scandalous dress that so-and-so wore to church, or someone else's unmarried pregnant daughter. My grandma would listen attentively, shaking her head with the occasional *tsk*.

Other than stolen pieces of conversation, sex was a taboo subject in my Italian grandparents' household.

The silence on this topic was also deafening in my Czech grandparents' country home in Michigan, which had previously belonged to my great-grandmother, "Baba."

During summer days, we kids roamed the woods while Grandma cooked and Grandpa gardened. A mélange of Dutch Masters, reheated coffee, burnt firewood, and Cashmere Bouquet soap permeated the house. The quiet, cool evenings were punctuated by the *MacNeil/Lehrer NewsHour* jingle and the 9:00 train whistle. We went to Church on Sundays, the laundromat on Tuesdays, and shopped on Fridays.

"Hell" was a bad word, and we only watched PG or below rated programs. When kissing scenes came on in *Laverne and Shirley*, Grandma denounced them as "dumb."

Days before my last full summer in Michigan, a boy kissed me at my eighth-grade graduation party.

I felt as though I had something to hide. Something ineffable had shifted. Maybe it was all the Judy Blume books I'd been reading, but I thought I should *look* different now. Would my grandparents detect this change? Overcome by the cloying notes of Cashmere Bouquet, I examined myself in the same mirror I had consulted at age nine, when my face was swollen from a bee-sting. I mechanically ran my grandma's heavy, gilded brush (that matched the mirror's frame) through my Princess Diana haircut.

I would return many times to that mirror, an inverted version of the fairy-tale Evil Queen's quest, searching for remnants of virtue: at fifteen when I double-pierced my ear, at seventeen when I was passionately in love, at nineteen in my first trimester of an undisclosed pregnancy, and at twenty-two as a *disgraced* divorcée.

Somehow, in that safe space, although everything had changed, nothing had changed.

In 2003 I traveled back to say goodbye to my dying grandmother and to the house that would soon be sold. I drank in the ghost smells of Sanka, cigars, and woodsmoke. My grandmother's caregiver had replaced the Cashmere Bouquet with liquid Dial, but the gilded mirror and brush remained. Fully aware of the ceremoniousness, I brushed my hair and gazed at my reflection. At thirty-four, I now sported a soccer-mom ponytail, was married to a Classics professor, and was ABD in Italian. Whether I had ever fallen from grace or redeemed my virtue was suddenly irrelevant. A new revolution had dawned, launched by femme fatales like Carrie Bradshaw who were smashing the unspoken code and embracing a holistic view of womanhood: one in which beestings and roller-skate scars were not incongruous with piercings or sensuality.

Twenty years later, in my own mirror, I still search for vestiges of youth. Instead, my reflection reveals creases and silver strands, assiduously earned—a profound virtue not defined by modesty.

Bernice Kotkin Myers

by PAT MYERS

I failed to appreciate my mother in the sixteen years she lived after I was born. Growing up with a single mother in the 1920s and 1930s, she was put into bad foster care because her mother couldn't afford to raise her. Not considered to be of the "college girl" class—even though she was highly literate, a voracious reader and crossword solver—she took the secretarial track at Olney High in South Philadelphia and worked in offices from the day she graduated in 1941.

By the time she finally married my father in 1954, she was considered shamefully overdue for marriage. She fantasized about those 1950s movie and TV housewives who stayed home and had cocktail parties. My father found that totally silly and felt she wasn't trying enough to improve herself. For example, having been a city dweller all her life, she was too nervous to learn to drive after they moved out to what was then the total sticks, a suburb that required a car. They simply were not compatible.

The one thing they both were crazy about was their little know-it-all child, born more than four years after they married (also considered a huge delay). I was the total focus of each of their lives.

My parents stuck it out for a while, misguidedly for my sake. They divorced when I was twelve, and I went with my mother when she moved from the DC area to Philadelphia's South Jersey suburbs (also extremely car-dependent). She began taking a commuter bus into the city for yet another secretarial job, coming home long after dark.

I was just entering adolescence and, alas, failed to show any maturity, compassion, or empathy during this miserable and isolated time of hers. She had no other friends besides me. Her health began to fail well before she turned fifty—high blood pressure, anxiety, and, I'm sure, undiagnosed depression, along with eventual kidney and other internal problems—and my mother was hospitalized several times. I did poorly in school, suffering from a string of vague ailments and not doing the work. I was about to flunk tenth grade when the school suggested to my father, who had remarried, that I move away to live with him and his family. I went down to Maryland for my usual summer sojourn, and never returned.

It was the literal kiss of death for my mother. She had nobody, and she was sick. She moved into the city and began to work again, until she couldn't. She died alone at age fifty-one, except for some elderly relatives. She would have been proud to know that I ended up in the word business, but in those last years, I wasn't there.

Bernice Kotkin Myers, 1924–1975.

Summer 1976

by LYNN PERIL

I have a crisp memory of Kim, dressed in flared denims and an army jacket, her dark brown hair cascading in marcel waves away from a center part, a scowl on her wide, pale face, walking toward me through the crowded hallway of Burleigh Junior High. She always seemed older than I, though in fact she was younger, tough in a way that I didn't understand. We were not friends. In fact, she scared me.

The school was a modern building set among rolling fields in Brook-field, Wisconsin, a well-to-do suburb west of Milwaukee. We had recently moved from the city, where I'd attended accelerated classes at 65th Street School.

There my classmates were smart and snarky, and we went on field trips and to science camp. I went to Cindy B's slumber party, where we watched Alice Cooper on *Don Kirshner's Rock Concert* and used a green Magic Marker to re-create his eye makeup on the first girl who fell asleep. (This proved more difficult than anticipated. Only a few pale stripes had been drawn on her twitchy lid before she woke up and joined in the general laughter.)

At Burleigh, people didn't care about their schoolwork. They ignored the teachers, talked through classes, and smoked in the bathroom I went from being in with the in-crowd to being an ungainly weirdo who cared about her grades, and I hated it.

I had always been a quiet, obedient child, but after two years at Burleigh, I'd had enough. I was done with the rowdy classes, the smoky bathrooms, the mean girls who whispered about "some people" just loud enough for you to hear. And so, the summer between eighth and ninth grades, I delivered an uncharacteristic ultimatum to my parents:

"I don't care what you do, but you'd better do it, and fast, because I'm not going back to Burleigh."

Which took nerve. My father was a World War II combat veteran, whose untreated PTSD meant that he often reacted with rage to the slightest provocation. I walked on eggshells around him, and yet I don't remember any yelling. I remember looking at ads for private schools—and then, that fall, I was on a school bus to a nearby parochial high school.

This was the story I believed and told others for years: I stood up to my parents, advocated for my rights, and was victorious. Going to the Catholic school was a turning point in my life, and one of the best decisions I ever made.

But something else happened that summer—an event I hadn't connected with changing schools until I recently revisited it with a newspaper search engine.

On July 2, 1976, two days before the Bicentennial, on a two-lane highway where the suburbs wound out into the countryside, Kim and three other girls from Burleigh were killed when the car they were riding in crossed over the center line and collided with a truck. The car's driver, a twenty-one-year-old man, also died. The truck driver survived, as did another girl in the car, also a student at Burleigh. One of the girls who died was fifteen, just like me. Kim was only thirteen.

Everyone in the car had been drinking. Two of the girls were legally drunk, even by the easygoing blood-alcohol standards of the '70s. An eyewitness said everyone was "laughing and singing and having a good time" as the car passed her house, tires squealing, moments before the collision.

I learned about the crash when I pulled the *Brookfield News* out of our mailbox the following week. The cover photo was stark: a sheet-covered body on the ground, a desert-booted foot sticking out. (At least this is how I remember it. I haven't been able to track down a copy to confirm.) Something about the boot or the body's small

73

stature made me think it was Kim under the sheet. Later, when I read *Lolita*, I thought of this photo when Humbert and Dolly, on the run, pass a highway accident and Dolly points to the victim's shoe and says it is the exact type of moccasin she'd unsuccessfully tried to describe to "that jerk in the store."

At fifteen, I was immortal; my parents might not have seen it that way. Maybe what I saw as their yielding to my demand was less about capitulation and more about that photo of someone's daughter, who could have been their daughter, who could have been me.

On Some Days

by JENNIFER RIZZO

When you're biracial you have a lot of guilt. Guilt that you're not more White. Guilt that you're not more Black. Guilt that you try to look White in high school by straightening your hair every morning or more Black by lying outside in the sun with bronzer on, turning your pale skin red. When I was in my late twenties, I was tired of people asking me if I was Latina. I took a 23andMe DNA test. Weeks later, I stared at the results on my phone as it broke down everything that quantified me. I looked in the mirror at my dark brown eyes, my calico pipe-curled hair, and the freckles scattered across my face. I wanted to be one thing or the other, because when you are both you are forced to choose sides. I grew up apologizing for who I was. I grew up in limbo. I was too ashamed to claim what I was, so I let a DNA test do it for me.

It was the third week of school when a student stopped and asked me, "What are you? You're too tan to be just White." Another student who had been in my class the year before replied instantly that I was biracial.

"Who is Black?" he replied instantly.

I numbly replied, like so many times before, "My dad. He was. He died."

I forgot the shock value that this response had. I watched his face as he pondered this.

"Was he a good dad?"

I paused. "On some days."

He nodded his head in understanding. I knew he had a complicated relationship with his father. As he read my face, we silently engaged in a mutual understanding not to continue the conversation. There is an awkwardness that happens between a teacher and student when teachers are revealed as being more than the subject they teach.

The problem with growing up with an alcoholic parent is that you tend to only remember the bad times. His birthday was September 22. He would have been sixty-six. I look at how I am now and attribute it to how he was as a father. I struggle with intimacy. I engage in emotional manipulation. I grieve to myself. Some days I wake up and my chest is tight and my head throbs. The air feels heavy, and it is hard to breathe. In the middle of the day, I go into the bathroom, cry, compose myself, and go back to living. This happens every September and October. September because it was his birthday; October because it is when he died. It is like two months of suffocation. PTSD and depression flow through my body like the arthritis that crawls up my thirty-three-year-old spine and across my hips—the aftermath of being body-slammed on my fifteenth birthday for screaming at my father to stop throwing my brother into the piano.

I wonder if shame is genetic. His father violently disowned him for being light-skinned. I look at the DNA results, the map of everywhere my blood is spread. Africa is lit up like a Christmas tree. I am made up of percentages: 39.1% French and German; 15.1% Scandinavian; 4.6% British and Irish; 1.0% Finnish; 8.1% Broadly Northwestern European; 67.9% White; 29.2% West African; 18.2% Nigerian; 6.3% Ghanaian, Liberian, and Sierra Leonean; 1.4% Senegambian and Guinean; 3.3% Broadly West African; 2.3% Congolese and Southern East African; 0.6% unassigned; 32.1% Black. It seemed like the DNA test had just as much trouble saying what I was as I did.

I stare down at my wedding ring, an heirloom from my husband's family.

When I was younger, I tried to break up with my now-husband. I warned him that I would push him away. I thought I was too broken and that I would take him down with me.

"You made a mistake. That boy is the best thing that has ever happened to you. He makes you happy," my dad told me from the living room couch, staring at me with his dark brown eyes, curly hair, and freckles scattered across his face like stars.

My dad taught me to accept the love that I deserve. He taught me that I was more than my percentages, my insecurities, and my confusions. More than his percentages, his insecurities, and his confusions.

Was he a good dad? On some days. Today is one of those days.

Paper Robes and Good Panties

by LISA DOUGLAS

There should be some kind of law about giving people bad news when they're wearing nothing but their good panties and a paper robe. Naked is naked, and good panties usually mean good things. Instead, I'm stuck here near-naked with a near stranger, hearing what could be the worst news of my life.

A lifetime of good behavior, good habits, and good hygiene was supposed to prevent me from ending up here with an abnormal pap smear, fresh from an ultrasound and a biopsy. I've never had unprotected sex; I've never had casual sex.

After a routine pap smear, my gynecologist found abnormalities; the doctor ordered an ultrasound. They found several growths on my uterus. This led to a biopsy.

I'm now waiting for the results.

My doctor is worried because I have been a fervent baby powder user, which increases the chances of those growths being cancerous.

Who would have thought that baby powder would be the real threat? Every day, twice a day since I was twelve, involved a liberal dusting on my lady parts after a shower. A perfect complement to a lady's toilette.

Given all of my good care and precautions, I assumed I could miss a few pap smears, but apparently not. The pretty-scented powder was a danger in itself.

The rest of the medical conversation went by in a blur of handouts, pamphlets, and follow-up appointments.

When you lead with "Possible cancerous growths," that's it. It closes the show. End scene. Everything else is just credits.

The fog that I felt in the doctor's office ended immediately as I stepped outside. Everything was suddenly new. The sun was brighter, the leaves were greener, the flowers more colorful. As if I was seeing everything for the first time, now that I knew it could be one of the last times, I wondered what else I hadn't seen or hadn't done. What else I had taken for granted.

I was hungry.

I went to Wendy's. It'd been years since I had fast food. I got the biggest sandwich they had, covered it in bacon, got a large Frosty, and ate it all in the car. I didn't care. I licked my fingers and scraped the cheese off the wrapper. I drained the cup dry. It was the greatest burger I'd ever had.

And as the sweet sticky liquid dribbled down my chin, I thought, *This is worth dying for.* Then I laughed at the irony.

I laughed until I cried. Until there was nothing left but the satisfaction of being full and the emptiness of uncertainty. I was falling into the unknown.

As I was sitting in that feeling, a little boy came up and tapped on my window.

I rolled it down, ashamed and embarrassed to be caught crying in public. I scrubbed my eyes with the back of my hands, and suddenly I was a child too. He handed me his kids' meal toy. It was some kind of rocket.

"You can have this one. I already have one." Then he ran off back to his mother.

I know lots of people want to go to Europe or to fall in love. They go shopping, or do any other crazy thing when they find out they are sick.

I've traveled and been in love; I have a closet full of clothes.

I just want to see my mom and my dad. I just want to curl up in my childhood bed and have someone tell me everything is going to be okay. I want to swim at the beach. I want to play with my nieces and nephews.

I pulled back through the drive-through, ordered four more giant sandwiches and three kids' meals. The cashier looked at me like I was crazy. My smeared makeup, my ketchup-stained face, and the Frosty on my shirt. I tipped her $20 and she seemed to understand.

My phone begins to ring. It's the doctor's office. And in that second I tell myself I'm only forty-two. I'll try every shark-fin experimental Slurpee out there. Koala-bear-platypus- squid drink? Fine. If there is some weird treatment, I'm trying it.

I answer the phone. I listen carefully. I'm sick, but I'm not dying. Not even close. It's fibroids.

I have to tell my family what's happening, so I'm bringing the best medicine I know. I hope there are more fast-flying rockets as prizes, to lift us all.

Roti-Making Dreams

by MADIHA SHAFQAT

Am I a fallen woman for not knowing how to make a perfect roti? According to my Ammi, yes, I am.

Making roti, a type of flatbread, is a very important part of Pakistani culture. If a woman knows how to make a perfectly round and puffed roti, she is the crown jewel of the family and the Pakistani community. This is an even greater achievement for the mother, who is praised for raising a daughter skilled in the art of roti-making. And as soon as I popped out of the birth canal on November 7, 1994, at 3:21 p.m. in Hartford, Connecticut, *Ammi* had a plan.

Since I was a wee baby, Ammi handed me a ball of dough in my chubby little hands and started training me in the art of roti-making. Some parents groom their children to become world-famous tennis players, others groom them to win spelling-bees; in my household Ammi was grooming me to become a perfect roti-maker. As I stood there, a toddler with sticky hands from the dough ball I was obliterating into tiny pieces, I could feel pride oozing out of Ammi. *She's a natural,* I remember her saying to Abbu. But time would prove that the only thing I was a natural at was being a rebel.

The first time Ammi entrusted me with a rolling pin was the day my brother got a huge bump on his forehead. Instead of rolling out the dough, I decided to play whack-a-mole with my brother—as an annoying five-year-old, my brother was very whack-able. I was banned from going near the rolling pin for years to come, but Ammi stayed resilient.

Next, Ammi tasked me with sifting the flour, but instead of sifting it over a bowl as instructed, I "made it snow" all over the kitchen. I could see a flicker of frustration on Ammi's face, but she wiped it away, deciding to soldier on.

I was ten when Ammi pulled me away from the TV and charged me with kneading the roti dough. "Put in some elbow grease," she said. To make it more interesting, I decided to bury "little treasures"—aka bedazzling jewels—deep into the dough. The dough was sparkly and colorful, which I deemed a success, but Ammi did not. Withered but still not willing to give up, Ammi pushed on.

At the age of thirteen, things took a turn for the worse when I almost burned the house down . . . not on purpose! I was helping Ammi cook roti on the stove and forgot to flip it. Billows of smoke rolled out of my charcoal-black sad excuse of a roti as Ammi hosed it down. I didn't just set a roti on fire that day, I also set fire to Ammi's dreams of my becoming a perfect roti-maker. The aftermath was not pretty. Ammi finally cracked; and in the heat of the moment, she told me I was a disappointment, that I was hopeless and could never be the crown jewel of the family. Those words stung deep. That was the last day I tried to make roti.

Until fourteen long years later, at the age of twenty-seven. As I sit in my Southern Californian apartment doom-scrolling, not being able to decide what to order on Grubhub, my stomach twinges for a taste of home, for a taste of Ammi's roti that I took for granted as a teenager. *Am I brave enough to tackle making roti on my own?* I have to give it a try, so I put my hair in a ponytail and get to work. I sift the flour like Ammi taught me to, then mix the water in. As I knead the dough, I hear Ammi's voice echo in my mind: *Put in some elbow grease.* So, I do. I push the plushy dough in and then pull it over. Back and forth. Back and forth. It is quite therapeutic. Then I make little dough balls that I flatten before it is time to cook them on the pan. Thankfully, my faulty roti-making skills do not lead to a fire this time around. Instead, to my surprise, my deformed roti actually puffs a tiny bit. Proud of myself, I take a picture and send it to Ammi, who "hearts" it immediately. Then my phone rings. It's Ammi. Joking, I ask her, "Am I a crown jewel yet?" Ammi replies, "Perfect roti or not, you have always been a crown jewel to me."

Beware of That Which Bites

by GRETA SCHEIBEL

On the edge of the rain forest in Panama's Darien Province sits a shack. The dirt floor is home to a colony of biting ants that attack any time you try to cross the room. At night, vampire bats enter through the gap between the walls and the roof, and if your feet are exposed, they will slice open the soft skin behind your toes, feed on your flesh, and leave you to bleed peacefully in your sleep.

This is where Drew lived.

Drew and I were old friends from camp, which means we had been everything from pen pals to bedfellows and, finally, good old friends. When he joined the Peace Corps after college, I couldn't wait to visit.

I arrived at Drew's shack in May 2007, during the start of the rains. I wanted to fit into his beloved jungle world, but I didn't expect to be eaten by it. Each time the ants attacked, they took tiny bites of my confidence with them as a sacrifice to their queen.

The second week, Drew and I went to visit one of his worksites further into the forest. At dawn I was transported over a mountain on the back of a donkey, not unlike minor royalty, to yet another shack. When we arrived, Drew left me in a hammock and went off to dig a ditch with a group of men.

It must have been a large ditch, because he was gone all day, which was enough time for me to get my period, grow miserable, and plan my escape to Panama City. We could hike to a highway, catch a ride to the city, and have a shower. It was a good plan, with strong incentives.

Drew disagreed. He pointed to the clouds and suggested that we leave in the morning. There would be fried pork and guitar music. I thought his was a bad plan, with weak incentives. Plus, I was bleeding; I knew the bats would get me.

I stood up and told Drew that I was going with or without him. Left with no choice, he reluctantly followed. As soon as we left, it began to rain. The path turned to mud that seemed to melt away with each step. Within an hour, we were soaked. Drew didn't speak to me, both because he was angry and because it was impossible to hear over the deluge.

As I crossed a mossy log, I looked to Drew for comfort. In his eyes I saw only fear. I felt ashamed. Had I listened instead of rushing headfirst into something I didn't understand, dragging Drew with me, we would be safe and dry. In the past, my strong will had gotten me through challenges. Now it had gotten me, and someone I loved, into one. Waste deep. And the only way out was through a swamp.

After six hours, we arrived at the final river crossing before the road. The sky was dark, and the water was deep. It roared as it rushed downstream. I could not cross by foot, and it was too wide to cross by mossy log.

Out of nowhere appeared a man on a horse. He said something to Drew, then gave me a leg up onto his horse. Slowly, the stranger ferried me across the angry river to safety, while Drew followed in his footsteps. Who was he? Where had he come from? Once we were on the other side, Drew and I stared, bewildered, as our savior disappeared back into the night.

Drew, a legend in his own right, forgave me quickly over a bottle of Pinot Grigio once we made it to the city.

Before I went to Panama, I imagined I was the hero of my own story: an independent woman who was ready to take on the world. In Panama I realized this was a fantasy. The real world had things that could bite, or wash me away, especially if I threw myself into them.

Luckily, the real world was also full of people who did know about these things. And I learned to listen to them.

When I think about Drew and Panama, I think of his shack. Where the wildness crept in. I think of how we are all like that shack, only superficially separated from our own wildness.

It's when we step out into the unknown that we discover our true nature: shortfalls, abilities, and all. It is worth the trip.

Do mind the bats, though. They bite.

When Your Friends Say, "*Ooh la la*"

by EMILY TOTH

The song made us giggle and blush.

It's about two teens who go to a movie. It's boring. They fall asleep—and when they wake up, it's 4:00 a.m.

"Our goose is cooked!" they howl. "Our reputation is shot!"

And "What are we gonna tell our friends when they say, 'Ooh la la'"?

That song, "Wake Up Little Susie," taught me to fear being a "Fallen Woman."

If a couple spent long hours alone in a passion pit like a car—well, everyone would assume they had "done it." The girl would be "ruined."

The song is jaunty—but it's told by the boy and sung by the Everly Brothers. If a young woman sang it, it might be different. And tragic.

What did youngsters actually "do" in the late 1950s, when the first baby boomers were coming of age? In my class at Lakewood (Ohio) High School, some girls were "fast." They wore tight clothes and leather jackets and looked like they were starring in *Grease*, which hadn't been written yet.

We didn't know that sexual "reputations" were about class. Girls from Birdtown (the immigrant ghetto) were said to be "looser" than the doctors' daughters from Clifton Park.

At class reunions, I've learned that many of the rich girls in cashmere sweaters also did it with their boyfriends—while we middle-of-the-pack girls followed the rules. No "all the way" unless you were at least engaged.

The specter of the Fallen Woman was about being bourgeois. It was about seeming respectable to the tut-tutters who have always spread the word that "one slip, and you're gone."

How bizarre, I think now. A woman's whole life gets rated by what she does—or what's done to her—with her private parts? What about her brain? Why can't she be seen as a doctor, a lawyer, a movie star, a journalist, a nun, a Realtor? We have all those in my high school class—and I don't know if they "fell" in their private lives.

If they did, they got right back up.

But that's not what our stories taught us. "Wake Up Little Susie," composed by Felice and Boudleaux Bryant, came out in 1957. Just a year after *Peyton Place*, Grace Metalious's notorious novel in which everyone does it—though the women often don't want to.

That's most true for the teenaged shack dweller, Selena, raped and pregnant by her stepfather. The town doctor performs an abortion (totally illegal) and makes an impassioned speech about her right to choose her future.

But her reputation is shot.

Her clean-cut boyfriend, who claimed he'd love her forever, suddenly figures out that having a notorious wife could wreck his promising career.

He dumps her.

The victim also gets blamed and shamed in Glendon Swarthout's *Where the Boys Are* (1960), the first spring break novel and movie. Horny college students cavort, get drunk, pair up. But I most remember a tearstained face. Yvette Mimieux plays the naive coed who's raped by a Yale man—because he heard she was "easy."

That was also the year, 1960, that the Pill came out. Women could go ahead and do it—but not really.

The old story, about reputation, lingers in our libraries and in our minds.

"Seduced and abandoned" was the top plot in nineteenth-century novels. It's the story of *The Scarlet Letter* (1850). It's also the tale of

Tess, the naive country girl in Thomas Hardy's *Tess of the D'Urbervilles* (1891). Raped by a rich, callous playboy, she tries to start anew. But her Nice Guy New Husband finds out she's "ruined."

He dumps her.

Peyton Place in its day was banned; *Where the Boys Are* was condemned. So was Hardy's *Jude the Obscure*, also about sexual blaming.

Nowadays religious fundamentalists still carry on about fallen women—though nearly half of American children are born to single mothers.

The Bible is also kinder than many of its thumpers.

In the Old Testament, Dinah is raped by the ruler's son (Genesis 30:21; 34; 46:15)—but she is not shamed or blamed. Instead, her rapist and his brothers are sentenced to be circumcised.

In the New Testament, the story of the woman taken in adultery (John 8) inspires Jesus to say, "Let him who is without sin cast the first stone."

Jesus's own mother, after all, was not married when she became pregnant. She must be the world's most famous fallen woman.

But we're not supposed to say that.

Or say, "*Ooh la la.*"

First Kiss

by JENNIFER SCHARF

My Jordache jeans are so tight that I lie on my bedroom floor, looking up at my pastel-colored unicorn dreamcatcher, and suck in my stomach as I zip and—one more breath in—button them. I got the jeans for my thirteenth birthday. My mom had to work overtime to get them for me, and I am determined to wear them until they fall apart. In middle school you need to look cool, and nothing else in my closet makes the cut.

I scribble a note for my parents, toss it on the kitchen table, and sneak out the back door. Waiting for me in the driveway is my friend's older sister, the epitome of cool. I can't believe she invited me to a high school party! I squeeze into the overcrowded red station wagon and sit on the edge of the seat next to some guy in a bow tie. I worry that maybe I don't look fancy enough: Should I have worn a dress? As we zip down the road, the smell of fruity wine coolers fills the air. My stomach turns. Everything about this feels wrong. When we roll up to the party, I'm in such a hurry to get out that I open the car door against the curb. It's dented. How could this night could get any worse?

The house is humming with people, everyone bigger and more adult than me. I don't know who to talk to, so I stay in the kitchen while a cacophony of music and bellowing laughter swirls around me. My bladder is burning from anxiety. I look around for a bathroom, and I'm in the hall when someone yanks my hand and pulls me into a dark room. For a split second, I think it's my friend playing a prank. Before I realize what's happening, I'm conscious of hearing the door lock, I'm tossed onto the bed, and a breathy and heavy body is over me, smothering me. I turn my head from side to side to avoid his mouth, warm saliva covering my cheeks. I'm not sure what a kiss is supposed to feel like, but I know it's not this. Whoever he is, I beg him to stop. I try to push him off of me, but he is too strong. I see him as a dark shadow grinding against me and feel his hands frantically trying to unbutton my jeans. My jeans that I thank God are too tight.

There's a knock on the bathroom door in the hallway, and suddenly he stops. Just like that, he gets up, unlocks the door, and walks out. I catch a glimpse of him and I recognize him; we rode over in the car together. He's the bow tie guy. That doesn't make sense. Why would someone in a bow tie do this to me?

I get up and turn on the light. It looks like the parents' bedroom, neat and tidy, with floral curtains that match the bedspread. There's a framed photo on the dresser, a wedding portrait; two smiling faces stare back at me. I think they would be furious if they knew we were in their pristine bedroom, doing . . . this. I smooth the wrinkles out of the bedspread and fluff the pillows. My bladder is still burning, and this time I find the bathroom, close the door behind me, lock it, and decide what to do. I'll tell my friend's sister what happened, and she'll take me home.

But she laughs and says I must be imagining things. And she's staying. She assigns a babysitter for me, a "really good guy" who isn't drinking. He's captain of the football team and has big hands and a red-and-white letterman jacket. He asks if I want to play Connect Four. I don't, but I nod. We're in the basement. Alone. As we play, I watch his hands intently, waiting for them to grab me and tackle me to the ground. I focus on the sound of the chips dropping into the grid. Click, click, click. As long as the chips keep falling, I must be safe. I don't feel safe, though. I just want to go home and lie on my floor and look up at my pastel-colored unicorn dreamcatcher. To forget. Or rewind. To be that girl who thought it was so cool to be invited to a high school party.

If this is what it feels like to be a woman, I never want to be one.

Sweet Tooth

by KYLIE RAMIA

Did you know that the craving for sweets is hereditary? My mom prefers to skip straight to dessert, and my dad has his favorite bakery on speed dial. And as their first child, I developed a sweet tooth that manifested into a force stronger than both of theirs combined.

The consequences as a kid were luckily mild. Countless fillings and flossing lectures were vexing enough, but who really knows how to properly floss as a six-year-old? I barely harbored the patience to stand on the bathroom stool with a toothbrush in my mouth for a full two minutes, leading to a hefty sum in dental bills—much to my parents' disappointment.

"Did you floss tonight?"

I lied through my not-so-flossed teeth, nodding to affirm.

The fib didn't survive long. Soon, my dad hovered next to me to ensure the fruition of my oral hygiene routine. Cavities were the bane of my existence, so I conceded and let him dictate.

When I was six, I had no idea that cavities were only the start to a long and grueling battle against my sweet tooth. My mom's weakness is cheesecake. My dad couldn't resist a good, old-fashioned chocolate chip cookie crisp out of the oven, even if he tried. Frankly, I never had much willpower when it came to either.

So, I indulged.

In Oreos, Rice Krispie treats, Ho Hos—remember Ho Hos? Those mini, cylindrical chocolate cakes with swirls of cream folded inside? I had one of those every day after school in the fourth grade. But Mom and Dad weren't fans. They watched over me like candy shop clerks, presuming I might steal from the pantry shelves at any given moment. And they didn't hide their apprehension, instead reframing their approach. Maybe if I feared the Ho Hos, sweets would become the enemy. Maybe I would fight the craving.

I struggled, knee-deep in battle with jeans while Mom peeked at the tag.

"You've just put on a bit of weight. We'll go buy more."

"Is that bad?" I asked hesitantly.

"No, we should just watch your weight."

She was looking out for me, obviously. I was advised three snacks per day. Then she bought me a scale. A thoughtful gift. Brush teeth, go pee, drop pants, step on, wait for number to stare back at me—as she hovered.

That number ruled my days.

Come middle school, my parents signed me up for the swim team. You know, because why not put me in a swimsuit while I'm battling body dysmorphia? And these swimsuits were ugly. Speedo one-pieces flattered *no one*. Don't even get me started on the *swim cap* and *goggles*. I had to wear that terrible triad for three years.

"Swimming will be good for maintaining your weight."

Thankfully, swim days were over by high school. Sweets never stopped being the go-to; neither did the scale. It was easy to go the entire school day without eating when there was no one to police you, followed by a regrettable feast when the hunger inevitably consumed you. The regret weighed in every morning. Added half a pound.

Dad often drove me to school.

"We only want you to be conscious of your eating."

"I understand," I reassured him.

"Good, good. You know, men prefer girls who are thin over girls who are . . . bigger."

More nods. Silence.

My mom was the infamous hoverer. She often picked me up from school.

"Wait, so you think I'm overweight?"

She rolled her eyes. "No, you're fine. Not thin, but fine."

I scoffed. She gave me a look.

"You want honesty from me, right?"

My sweet tooth never waned, only sharpening over the years. I started to crave more than what I could eat.

And I didn't fight it.

I wanted deliciously decadent things. Snacks my parents couldn't track. The first time I succumbed to new cravings was in an old Mercedes with a guy I hardly knew. The second time, an SUV. A guy I knew even less so. I was seventeen. In need of sugar, more than just a sample.

So I indulged in sweets that never fully satisfied, flavors that only sat on the tongue for so long. Without the hoverers, I was free to indulge as I pleased. For years.

When presented with a treat, I almost never refused. But . . . sometimes I did.

Once, it was forced down my throat anyway.

And why wouldn't the sweet tooth *want* sugar, right?

Bet Mom and Dad didn't see that one coming.

Hope and Pain

by MEREDITH TIBBETTS

I was thirty-four, standing over a sink in my bathroom, washing blood from my sweatpants, deciding whether to go to the hospital. The first time this happened, I was doubled over in excruciating pain, hoping the water would wash away the blood and the emotional trauma hitting me in debilitating waves of nausea.

It did not.

The second time, I was more prepared. I was warned a few days prior, during a checkup in a dreary room at a fertility clinic, that the chance of the pregnancy proceeding was about 50 percent.

I was pursuing parenthood alone, though with full support of my parents and siblings, opting to walk the path into the rarely discussed world of donor conception. To an outsider, it's flipping through glossy pages of exemplary men, picking out qualities you like, trying the "turkey baster" conception, and then—pop!—out comes a little infant Einstein.

It's not *quite* like that. Medical tests determine if you're fertile; psychologists make sure you aren't insane. (Clinics describe this mandatory session as "making sure you're prepared for the challenges ahead.")

More medical tests follow.

Remember that burst appendix you ignored that almost killed you a few years ago? Let's see if that scar tissue is blocking any necessary parts for conception.

Then you select a donor through an online database at select cryobanks. After choosing the eye color, height preference, college degree status, hair type, CMV status, and looking at childhood photos (adult photos cost extra), listening to a voice sample, and reading essays by the donor, you open PDF after PDF of medical information.

If my kid is going to be disadvantaged in the eyes of society as being from a one-parent family, it's going to start off as medically perfect as possible. Already stuck with my issues, why burden the new person with more—if I could avoid it?

I was convinced my first IUI (intrauterine insemination; a step up from the turkey baster) would work. I was young, had no health issues, and was active on the local swim team. IUIs are quick procedures—I went into work right after my morning appointment.

A few hours later, I was crying in the bathroom because the pain was so intense. The fertility clinic nurse assured me that to be a little uncomfortable was ordinary. A little uncomfortable? Lady, I didn't cry at work when an organ ruptured inside my abdomen; don't tell me "Everything's fine."

A few visits later, a fertility doctor surmised that the pain from that failed IUI was from sperm that hadn't been properly de-thawed before being released.

Fun!

The second IUI didn't work either.

What no one tells you is that every failed attempt breaks your heart a little bit. You start to lose confidence in yourself, even if you know that the chances of getting pregnant right away are slim. Why isn't your body capable of flipping off the statistical mean? Why isn't your body the special one?

The third IUI attempt resulted in a pregnancy. I saw the baby in the ultrasound; I heard the heartbeat. I graduated from the fertility clinic to an OB-GYN at eight weeks.

Then, when I was supposed to be just past eleven weeks pregnant, a doctor told me there was no heartbeat; my baby had died about a week earlier. It's called a "missed miscarriage"—your body doesn't recognize that the baby has died. I scheduled a D&C surgery to remove the fetus, but that night I found myself bent over my bathroom sink in the most pain since that burst appendix. At the emergency room with my father,

I told the receptionist I was having a miscarriage, back hunched over, my arm wrapped around my abdomen, tears streaming down my face.

My fourth attempt failed. My fifth resulted in a pregnancy that lasted seven weeks. My sixth failed. I was told to move onto IVF (in vitro fertilization) at that point, but I had one more vial of sperm left. If I was about to sink $25k into one round of IVF—with about a 30 percent chance of getting pregnant—I wanted to go into it with a clean slate and new sperm. I tried the seventh IUI.

I gave birth to my daughter three days past my due date.

The next time I went to an urgent care clinic involved an incident where my three-year-old's sparkly wand magically whacked my nose. I'm holding tissues, soaked red. Motherhood? It's been worth every bloody moment.

POP Star

by SARITE KONIER

"What's wrong?" my husband asked, going from confusion to concern as he caught me with a mirror between my legs.

I couldn't find the words. How could I tell him that my pelvic organs were oozing out of my vagina like a Salvador Dali painting?

My life was good, but as an older mom of a young child, this was far from the glitzy image I had in mind when I moved to LA in my twenties. I was peeing dribbles at a time, forced to preemptively go before every drive and again at our activities. I hadn't been able to successfully wear a tampon since childbirth, which meant a week each month of no pool time with our daughter. In Southern California. And now this!

An online search yielded pelvic organ prolapse (POP) images. I felt empathy for the cows on *The Incredible Dr. Pol*. Would a long, ungloved hand have to reach in to shove everything back? Cue the tears. *So that was the lump I felt in the shower.*

"Do you want the surgery?" asked the urogynecological surgeon. "I've done fifteen thousand of these—every Tuesday and Thursday." Thankfully wearing gloves, he gently pushed everything back in with a pessary, but I still needed a hysterectomy, my bladder moved up, my urethra straightened out, my vaginal vault lifted, and ligaments stitched back into place.

This was not exactly interior decorating of the stars.

I felt like a failure. While my husband and I had decided prior to this that our child would be our one and only blessing, my heart ached knowing that now I couldn't. My womb had been my baby's home for nine months. What were they going to do with it, anyway—discard it like a washed-up actor?

And I was embarrassed to admit to more than a hysterectomy. Only a trusted few knew what was *really* happening. I didn't expect my picture on a tabloid with the caption: "Her vagina is falling! Her vagina is falling!" But no one I knew had ever gone through this, and I felt grotesque and undignified.

And yet, doesn't everyone in LA get *something* done? My sagging jowls and graying hair suddenly didn't seem so bad.

Leading up to my surgery, the pessary popped out and the discomfort intensified. The once-internal skin grew sensitive and irritated from rubbing against my underwear, and even pushing a grocery cart created pressure from my pelvis down through my thighs. I started to ration standing activities; ordering delivery instead of cooking dinner bought me precious playtime with my daughter. Already, by late afternoon, I felt a heavy, dragging sensation in my abdomen and lower back, as though I were in the third trimester. My husband did whatever he could to support me, but this situation was only the curtain; backstage were pandemic lockdowns and increased work hours in preparation for his upcoming three weeks of family leave.

A year later I planted pomegranate seeds in our yard, using the most uterine-looking of the fruits I could find. If I couldn't grow another human, maybe I could at least grow a fruit-bearing tree? Alternatively, maybe I could outgrow my shame and share my experience so that other women would know they're not alone. And I wouldn't need a red carpet to do it. I could join online forums, talk with friends, write about it.

These days, I don't let much stop me. I cook, I clean, I run errands, and while I might still hesitate to jump or run, most days you can find me dancing with my daughter and singing at the top of my lungs without fear.

But I can't shake the feeling that it shouldn't have to be this hard. No one prepares us for these things.

Obviously, I would've had my daughter even if I'd known, but I just wish that in sex education books, or at our first gynecological visit, or even in female PE classes, someone would teach us the exercises we need to strengthen our pelvic muscles long before we're pushing a small human through them. By the time you attend a birthing class, finally learning to do sets of Kegels, it's already too late. We deserve better. A woman's body is capable of performing miracles; at the very least we should be able to live a life of poise without having to wear Poise. It's not a showstopping revelation, but it would still feel glamorous!

The Toxic Friend

by JESSIE LUBKA

Figuring out who you are as an adolescent? Troubling and tiresome for you and everyone around you. In high school, one wrong move and your social life appears to be burnt to ashes. Adolescent girls navigate four years of gossip, drama, and betrayal. While nobody has it easy, cliques of girls can roam the school hallways like apex predators, searching out their own kind to torment and savage. Expressions of individuality mark you as easy prey when cliques are the norm; being part of a group makes it harder to be winnowed from the herd and attacked. It's like you can be camouflaged because you all blend into one creature.

But here's what people rarely discuss: It is almost impossible to ween yourself off the magic juice if you're finally brought into the holy circle of popularity. Just like the animal kingdom, there is always a lioness commanding the pride. There is one leader calling the shots and deciding who is worthy of her presence.

Relationships from high school were some of my most meaningful experiences—both helpful and hurtful. The best of my friends from that time remain the friends they were then.

But the singular toxic relationship I had did not appear poisonous until the clock struck midnight and the spell wore off. I'd fooled myself into thinking everything was fine and so became, gradually, too blind to see how I was being treated—too thankful to have been welcomed into the "popular" clique, too innocent to see that what rested beneath the big blue eyes and perfect smile was nothing but manipulation and selfishness.

"Toxic" is a word associated with "death," "lethal amounts of harmful substances," "poison," and this person—the chokehold she had on the gaggle of pretty, skinny, insecure girls and the fear she instilled in those attempting to enter her gravitational pull—could be the textbook illustration of the emotional version of "toxicity."

Yet years later, I realized that I owe that relationship a thank-you note. Here goes:

Dear Former Friend,

I never thought you'd deserve my gratitude, but you do. Your selfishness, backhanded compliments, and condescending comments allowed me to avoid people like you in adulthood. Your remarks lived with me for many years before I was able to see that they weren't true. Your personality was built on insecurities—if you couldn't be perfect, no one could. The saddest part is that you were close to magazine-perfect. Your smile could shine brighter than the stars, and you could have brought so much joy—but you didn't. Instead you decided to be vindictive, vicious, and manipulative. Your corrosive bitterness undermined the confidence of those who wanted only your approval.

Your validation was sweet, but the foundation of your friendship was based on power and pressure, leaving behind unsavory emotional abuse. I was never going to be pretty or funny or skinny—I was going to be in the background forever, while you got to be the radiant light. No one—not me, and not any of the other girls in your orbit—would amount to anything with you by our side.

Your constant need for attention was fueled by putting others down, telling me I was unmemorable, then pointing and laughing. I would have never been anything standing in your shadow, that's for sure. But I'm not made to stand in the dark. I am meant to have my own story, not to be an ancillary character in yours.

The pain you caused did hurt for a long, long time. Your words weighed on me, and held me down, like an anchor falling through the ocean. I couldn't shake your pronouncements about my future: "You'll never be memorable," you declared, and "You've changed for the worse." I changed for the worse because I stopped living my life according to you. At sixteen, I was finally figuring out who I wanted to be. I was supposed to follow you, trust you, and never deviate from your plan. But I did, and that enraged you. "What would you be without me?" you asked.

Here's my answer, old friend:

I'm independent, selfless, and supportive. I'd drop everything if someone needed my help. I'm memorable for my sense of humor, wit, and intelligence. In part, these strengths are the result of being belittled for seven years by you and your herd of less-sturdy victims.

Your toxic friendship inoculated me against others like you. For that, I am in your debt.

Always,

A Strong and Confident Woman

Imagine a Better Way

by MELISSA LLARENA

I would rather torture myself for an hour and forty minutes, repeating the same words over and over, to nail a podcast than toil over a hot stove. What mom would admit that? It's not in our script. Are our individual desires supposed to die when we become a mom? The day I gave birth to my son, my mom whispered, "Welcome to the club. The Mom Club." Whatever selfish pursuits I wanted would have to be saved for another lifetime. Maybe my son would have to fulfill my dreams instead. Neither option sounded right for me. There was no way I would tie my future to some words on a script written for someone else. My imagination is too powerful. It's helped me solve big challenges. The truth is, I already knew a little about being a mom from when I was a little girl. I didn't like how it felt.

My mom was diagnosed with bipolar depression when I was two years old. Several times I was alone with her when she experienced the incredibly volatile highs and lows of her mental illness.

By thirteen, I was already thinking on my feet. My imagination was my sidekick. I used it to figure out how to not cause a scene in my neighborhood and how to keep sight of Mom without her seeing me. One day, I followed her into our local movie theater. I had to be creative. I let the movie attendants know that I was looking for my mom, and they let me follow her into a dark theater playing *The Last of the Mohicans*. She was imagining herself to be in touch with her native Taino roots. It's not that my mom had an active imagination; she had lost any sense of realistic limitations when she was under a manic spell. These were the challenges that trained my imagination and fostered my self-belief. How could I stop using my imagination now as a mom?

It all started when my plan to return to work fell apart after birthing my firstborn. My childcare arrangements disappeared overnight. I inhaled, quit on my first day back, and felt like I had tossed my MBA in the trash. I created my online coaching business instead. Then, one day, my husband told me about a James Altucher podcast episode where Gary Vaynerchuk challenged listeners to launch a podcast. He offered to be the #4 guest. James then offered to be a guest too. I felt a gush of "this is a dare." I imagined I had to do it. What could be more unexpected and crazier than not settling into my "mom role" in Fancy Town, Connecticut, and instead, launching a podcast with both Gary and James as my big-name guests? It took one hundred days, sixty-seven thousand words, and reheated rice and beans, but James was my fifth guest and Gary my tenth.

This podcast creation thing is something I wasn't prepared for, but I wasn't prepared for mothering three sons either. Who says you need to feel prepared for anything? You don't need to follow the preconceived conventions for any role in life.

One late afternoon, there I was—this mom on the hook to write a one-thousand-word article by that night who also had a Skype appointment with a former client, now my podcast coach. The plan was to record my intro and audio, both thirty seconds long. I wasn't in a podcast studio. I was kneeling at the foot of my bed. Sometime during the process, I had perched my laptop on my armoire, helping me to keep my spine straight. I already felt wiped out after a long day and, halfway during this grueling process, my back was killing me. "Nope. Let's do that again," said my former client for the twentieth time. I didn't slur, but an hour in I was desperate. I knew I had it in me. There are moments that require us to decide who we will be, and that mic moment was mine. My podcast meant I was putting my imagination to good use. That was the beginning.

We play many roles in life, not just as a parent. My imagination grew stronger because my mom could not use hers to the fullest. I've always been able to take what was in my imagination and create what excited me most in the real world. My imagination had been the most reliable friend a girl could ever have. It is my superpower.

Mother 28

by LAURA POPE

Nearly four decades of *shoulds* steadily pelting the ground around me. Years of advice, expectations, and equations for life raining down from trusted mentors and well-intended friends. I've gathered each one in my arms and neatly lined them up on a shelf, like little trophies. I've exhausted myself pursuing them, sure that they were the keys to a successful life. "You should focus on school, you should work hard and save, you should live here, travel there, be independent, settle down—and then your dreams will come true." I've spent my entire life believing this equation should work. Everyone said so.

And then one rainy Saturday morning, after a lifetime of waiting for the all-powerful *shoulds* to yield the beautiful life they'd promised, I broke. I sat in silence while a sweet friend held my gaze; and with tears racing down my cheeks, I quietly sobbed out the words that felt like admitting failure: "It should've been different than this." I steeled myself for her response, sure that she would join the chorus of friends and family and add yet another expectation to the pile. Instead, she paused, whispered my name, and then upended my perspective with one painfully disarming sentence: "You are worth chasing the thing that sets your soul on fire."

That day I finally understood just how many of my dreams I'd buried, just how much of myself I'd given up in pursuit of other people's expectations. It was a day soaked with intense joy and cavernous grief. I felt laughter bubble up and freedom expanded in my chest as I crawled out from under the weight of those *shoulds* and shook off the dust. I felt the deep sadness and regret break me open as I gazed down at the sacred pile of dreams I'd abandoned. I celebrated a chance at a new beginning, and I grieved a life I'd never gotten to live.

I could've stood there forever, stoically watching the dust settle over that mountain of expectations, reveling in the beauty of my newfound perspective. Instead, I cautiously scooped up my most precious dream, cradled it in my arms, and listened as my heart whispered, *You should try.*

Six months later, on a sunny January morning, I settle myself at my desk, launch my inbox to begin work for the day, and nearly burn my tongue on my second mug of coffee. Buried in the middle of ten neatly stacked new emails is the one I've been anticipating for weeks: my adoption agency update. After years of believing that everyone else's *shoulds* would lead me to motherhood, I am finally pursuing the one dream I've wanted since I was eight years old: I'm forging my own path and adopting.

I exhale deliberately, open the message and read, "Hi, Laura, good to hear from you! When I filter for those seeking similar matches, you're up to number 28!" The words sweep through me like wild freedom. *I am twenty-eighth on my agency's adoption waitlist.* I have a chance to become a mother.

Virgins and Sluts: Then and Now

by JOYCE SALTMAN

Back in the late 1950s—when we had all the great music, songs with words we could sing (and still remember), and proper attire, which included pearls (sometimes real), stockings (seams straight), and girdles (nothing could jiggle or bounce)—there were only two types of girls: sluts and virgins.

I was expected to be a virgin. Mom taught me, very early on, that "nice girls" were not permitted to "sleep" with men to whom they were not officially, formally, and publicly married. These terms were nonnegotiable.

If you lost your virginity or gave into some man's sexual urges, or, even worse, gave into your own, it would mean you were ruined, the way a piece of fruit would be spoiled. You'd become something to discard, or at least offer at a deep discount. You were supposed to remain in your original wrapping, with everything intact and showing no signs of being handled by somebody who wasn't ready to commit to taking home the whole package, in a nonreturnable white dress.

I did not have a single close girlfriend who was not a virgin. So, is it a big surprise that most of us got married the day after college graduation? We held out and kept our knees together as long as we could. We'd been seeing our boyfriends for years, holding hands, necking, petting, groping, and doing everything we could without doing IT.

IT would have changed our lives, we were warned, and the girls I knew were afraid of the threat hidden beneath that warning.

What would have happened if Marty, my boyfriend who became my first husband, and I had done IT during the seven years we dated before that fateful wedding day? Would I have been some kind of a "tramp"? Would I suddenly transform into a slut overnight, or in the middle of the afternoon, or whenever?

Would he have thought less of me? More frightening still, would *I* have thought less of me?

Would the world be able to tell what I had done? Would my mother know?

It certainly was not that I hadn't dreamed of feeling him inside me. Marty and I had shared a bed together during special out-of-town events that required getting a hotel room to attend. At those times, I slept under the covers; he froze on top of the covers. That's how brainwashed we were. I longed to feel our skin touching, breathless at the thought of being against each other without sheets and blankets and clothing between, but knew I'd never be able to face my folks if I wasn't a good girl.

So instead I joked that I planned to sprint out of the wedding venue with Marty as soon as dessert was served, but instead I ended up watching the crew putting the chairs on the tables after the guests left. That's how petrified I really was about losing my virginity to my high school sweetheart, who was a virgin himself.

Many of those early marriages were dissolved, proving that the sex drive alone cannot be the glue that keeps a couple together for life. However, the one part of our marriage that was not problematic was the sexual aspect.

When my "practice marriage" ended after fifteen years and two kids together, as a responsible adult, I was able to make new decisions for myself. Could I now become a wild woman?

At first, the transition to the life of a divorcée was difficult. I was not really prepared for a world of one-night stands or casual sex. The need for safety and commitment kept me in a comparable lifestyle to the one I had practiced while single. I soon remarried and had a wonderful life, until cancer left me a widow.

Finally, after several years, I became a fallen woman, and allowed myself to sample some more of life's delicacies in the form of sexual escapades with new men. Three years ago I met a delightful man with whom I shower together every morning and return to bed for the morning activities. I am stretching the boundaries, loving every daily sexual encounter, and even initiating sex on occasion—something no "nice girl" would have considered back in the old days in Brooklyn. My H.E. (Husband Equivalent), with affection and a certain amount of awe, calls me a "sex maniac." He insists she was always there within me, just waiting to be let out. She's not falling. She's flying—and smiling.

Taking Off

by AMY HARTL SHERMAN

"You work three days. You're off four. You call that a job?"

"Yes, Dad. I wish I was senior enough for a three-day week. I work hard enough. And while I'm grateful you were a workaholic, that's not my goal."

I was hired as a flight attendant by American Airlines right after graduating from the University of Illinois. Outstanding, right? Except that to my family, I was "just" a flight attendant.

It's tough coming from a family of engineers and science-brains. Mom majored in Mechanical Engineering at Cornell, getting her degree in three years because of World War II. Dad got an Electrical Engineering degree from Pratt Institute. One brother is an engineer at IBM. Just for laughs, I'm also related to George Westinghouse—the one who invented air brakes for locomotives. Oh, and my middle name is Frances, after a Great Aunt who worked on the Manhattan Project. I missed the genes coded for nuclear development and railway science, but I was given other gifts.

I have a sense of perspective, an admiration for all kinds of people, and, most importantly, a sense of humor. I also had the first and only union card and union job in my immediate family. Not exactly a white-collar dream, but that union was the reason being a flight attendant became a career instead of a brief adventure you signed up for until you turned thirty or, God forbid, got married.

There are plenty of assumptions about flight attendants, but being brilliant isn't the first one that comes to mind. I am aware. None of which had anything to do with wanting an interesting job that took me places, provided great opportunities to travel, and did not involve bringing work home. That's why, when the acceptance letter from American Airlines arrived on Christmas Eve 1977, my heart was soaring from that moment on. Bye-bye temporary job in accessories at Lord & Taylor. Hello, excitement. Hello, dream. It didn't matter to me what anyone thought. This was the one thing I was sure of in my life.

Growing up traveling with my family had, ironically, sealed the deal. When a flight attendant spilled a carton of milk all over me on our family trip to Hawaii, I was enthralled. No crying over spilt milk when your server is beautiful and wearing a muumuu. This flight attendant remained gracious as she apologized and tried cleaning me up. This remarkable creature was actually talking to me! A skinny thirteen-year-old who looked like Ernie from *My Three Sons*. She worked one flight from Chicago and then stayed over in Hawaii? Tell. Me. More.

My parents? They were all about education. Dad went to college because his older brother insisted. His parents dug up the money they had buried in the dirt basement to help. (They were from Germany and didn't trust banks.) Pratt Institute changed his life. He claimed it saved him from poverty; he was the poster boy for the traditional American Dream. Naturally, he and my mother wanted to make sure all of us had college degrees, for which I'm grateful.

But it was their love of travel that hit me right in the heart. My soul romanticized flying. I needed adventure. I wanted to be able to afford all of it. I had found my place, and it was above the world, in the sky.

Flying was never boring. Beyond the actual job, the benefits were everything. I always said, "I love my job on my days off." I mean . . . people . . . they can be great, or they can blow up in your face like an atomic bomb (right, Aunt Frances)? But I met fascinating people working with different crews every month; I was able to see my siblings, who lived all over the country; and I could afford to live in the heart of Chicago. If our uniform had included the iconic flight attendant cap, I would have tossed it in the air, à la Mary Tyler Moore.

I will forever be proud of being "just" a flight attendant. Traveling was "just" the icing on the cake. I took myself places and, along with my family, became thoroughly proud of my job.

When I told my grandmother (on the Westinghouse side) that I was going to be a flight attendant, she cautioned me to "be sure to pay attention to female passengers, not just the businessmen."

"Don't worry, Grams; I'd never do that. I'll be an equal opportunity bitch." And a very happy one at that.

When Will Enough Be Enough?

by KELSEY TYNIK

My neck is forward, my jaw is slightly ajar, and I'm biting the air.

I want that carrot, the one that's been dangling in front of me for years.

I aimed for it when I was applying to college. It was a shiny orange temptation with fluffy green leaves. It screamed success. The day I was accepted, I took a bite; it instantly grew back into its full juicy form. During all four years of college, I wanted another taste. Sometimes it was dangling close, only to become, on other days, impossibly far away. My carrot mocked me, offering a recipe of dreams that might never appear on my plate.

How will I graduate with the highest GPA? Will anyone care about an artist's GPA? Will my boyfriend still call me after we graduate? Is my artwork good enough? How will I make money? Will I find a job? Will I have to intern? Why the hell did I study illustration? What is wrong with me?

No one asked me for my GPA, ever. After much persistence, I got an internship. *You will have to intern.* Dressed in my New York City best, I took the New Jersey Transit Line to my new job at a glamorous office. After the fourth hour of unpacking dusty boxes in a prop closet, I took my lunch break, and cried to my mom on the phone.

Despite my tears, landing the internship meant I got a bite.

How will I move out of my parents and into New York? When will I stop being someone's bitch at work? How can I afford rent? Oh my God, I have to pay for gas and electric?! How do you kill a cockroach? What if there are mice? How will I get to work every day? Wait, health care costs HOW much?!

I made it out of my parents' house. But the bitchwork never stopped—it just dressed in new clothes. Turns out cockroaches aren't too hard to kill. Turns out you could adopt a cat to solve your mice problems. I went to the ASPCA. My cat was my first dependent, my first real bill, and a solution to my mice problem.

Will I hate Brooklyn? My apartment in Manhattan is closer to my parents. What will I do without my old super? Do I really have to take two trains to work? When will I ever date anyone again (my college boyfriend stopped calling me)? How will I make it in the art world?

Orange dreams and temptations still dangled beyond my nose.

Will I hate Queens? Will my studio be big enough for all my artwork? Will I be able to juggle nannying and studio time? Will I have better health care? Will I meet anyone in the art world? Will I ever not date a loser?

The outer boroughs share a secret sisterhood of single women, living alone, taking multiple trains to work, and possessing an ability to go so ballistic on any creep that crosses them that he would be the one crying and fleeing. My art studio had two windows. I made it to a job where I gave out the bitchwork. I went back to nannying for the comfort of health care and a flexible schedule. I spent every free minute fostering an art community.

I made work, fell in love, broke up, all the typical and corny stuff you do when you're young and living on your own in New York.

Will I hate being back in Connecticut? Will graduate school be worth it? Will my artwork improve? Will my New York art community forget about me? My health care will be amazing. Will my new relationship survive long distance?

Chomp

Will I ever show in New York again? Will I make it to print? Will I ever get press? Will I be unhappy to be back in Brooklyn? How will I feel finally cohabitating with a partner? Will my career suffer when I have kids? When will we move out of the city? Will I ever have a studio with four windows again? Will my community forget about me when I leave Brooklyn (again)? Will anyone care about my work?

I am still reaching and moving forward, jaw slightly ajar, asking questions. My hope is that I'll recognize success when it arrives.

But what I know now, even as I rise, and even as I am proud of my accomplishments, is that I haven't yet finished my vegetables.

Mollycoddle

by BOBBIE ANN MASON

From the deck I could see the dog running figure eights in the backyard, leaping over the stonework—piles of potential decorative wall that Mort had promised to finish before getting distracted by an ambitious balustrade project to be constructed of bamboo. Bamboo is surprisingly strong, he had asserted. He was chewing a flat toothpick. The dog was happy as long as he was loose. It is the hardest thing to see a dog unhappy, but when he is happy, he tugs the heartstrings and makes me happy too. I love dogs. Mort ignores my dog. He has a one-track mind. He loves launching—a new project seems to spring from his mind like a dream. More like a wet dream, in my humble opinion. He launches and then dissolves.

"You mollycoddle that dog," Mort said to me this morning.

"I'd rather mollycoddle than cuddle oddly," I said recklessly.

He looked at me funny.

I poured puddles of pancake batter on the outdoor griddle. It wasn't hot enough, and the batter just sat there in a stupor.

Mort was talking to the dog. I thought he said, "Put some paprika on that chick." They were too far away for me to catch their conversation. "You can't mollycoddle a corpuscle," Mort seemed to say. I thought he was giving the dog advice on women, as in you can't live with them or without them.

Dumping his resentments of me onto the dog was very unfair to the dog.

I untied the strings of my apron. *Why was I here?*

I felt that an ambitious sojourn, a leave of absence, was not out of the question. The dog is my role model. My figure eights might cover all of California.

How to Scramble the Egg

by SYDNEY MELOCOWSKY

My seventh birthday. I was at an amusement park. Children's shrieks speared eardrums. The sky was so blue it seemed artificial, as if it were custom-designed by the theme park itself. A few sporadic clouds observed the fast-paced thrill from a place of safety above. Mothers spent too much money. Fathers' enormous bellies boasted themselves from beneath poorly-buttoned Hawaiian shirts. The sun's rays dazzled off steel roller coasters. Its glare blinded the patrons waiting in far-too-long lines for a sweat-covered seat on a two-minute ride.

The park was a man-made attraction in the-middle-of-nowhere Massachusetts. This was the adrenaline seeker's paradise, the daredevil's heaven; it created something grandiose out of colorful plastics and metal reinforcements. To make the moment last, I decided to make my own fun: a game of truth or dare. In the spirit of thrill, I chose dare.

I dare you to hit your head once—as hard as you can—against that fire hydrant.

By my logic, the dare would be done in less than ten seconds, whereas I would forever mock myself for being "too scared" if I didn't. I counted down:

Three.

Two.

And closed my eyes.

One.

When I opened them, I expected to be in excruciating pain, but I wasn't. But the green bushes began to look blurry. Then they had no color at all. I slurred a call for help.

I didn't hear an answer before collapsing onto the hot pavement.

I reawakened in an ambulance to a stranger's voice instructing me to vomit into a clear bag if I felt the urge. No one asked me to do anything more than to aim. Nausea aside, I was content; I had no responsibility other than to allow trained responders to take care of me. I had an excuse to do nothing: I was missing half my forehead.

Now I'm not. I lift my index finger and caress the place where my split skull became a scar. It's faded. People consider me lucky that the only evidence of that day exists as a delicate horizontal line and a hazy memory. But as papers pile up and work shifts demand coverage, I sometimes wonder what might happen if my head were to conveniently split again. An accident.

No one would dare ask me to mend it just to meet a deadline. No one would think I was making excuses for incomplete essays. They wouldn't have to know what really happened. They only had to see the resulting mess, the splattered egg—not the scrambled one that led me there. It would be sleight sabotage to evade life's pressure without becoming a failure: a "technical difficulty."

It's tempting because it sounds too simple. But that's not how I imagine myself: my brain an exposed yolk whose potential lies in shards. I refuse to break so easily.

Yet there's a crack in my conviction.

But you're useless.

Stop. I know that isn't true. I need to be nicer to myself.

No, really. I don't say this to just anyone. You really are special because you truly have nothing to offer.

My heart is screaming, but my mouth remains shut.

I'm the strongest part of your brain. The rest of you is negligible. You simply need to erase all the unnecessary feed. Delete it all! What you feel now is all there is.

Sometimes I consider it a good option just to get rid of *her*. Unfortunately, she and I are inextricable. We ride together or not at all.

I imagine the other kids at the park that day have grown up. We are all adults quaking with the same apprehension as the versions of ourselves from years ago. We have always been barely tall enough to ride. We wait in line, day after day, while time ticks away in measured heartbeats. It's anxiety inducing. Our inhibitions begin as whispers, only to become louder as we arrive at the metal platform.

Tasks always looks more manageable before we have time to complete them. Having children seems exciting before we notice how unprepared we are to become parents. Our lives feel purposeful before we question our adequacy.

But arrival means beginning. It means taking a step and recognizing that we fear the anticipation more than the actual ride. We can smash our skulls in hope that the world stops with us, or we can fasten our safety belts and prepare for the coaster's climb.

How I Escaped Mom's Voice

by JOAN SEIGLER SIDNEY

No birth control worked. I tried everything. With four kids, I still wanted a career. My mother considered me "a fallen woman."

Mom and I sit bickering at my kitchen table, her blue eyes unflinching.

"Your husband and children are enough. Stuie makes a good living as a math professor. Why should you go to work?"

"Because I earned a Master of Arts in Teaching at Harvard."

Mom gets up to boil water. "Do you want tea?"

"Sure." I watch her set out cups, small plates, and *hamantaschen*. She's so capable, an assistant pharmacist trained in Lwow, at an elite *Gymnazium* for Jewish girls. Is this how she used her degree? I want to do more with mine.

"Mom," Stu interjected from the couch, eavesdropping. "You used to tell relatives, 'Joanie's a born teacher.' What changed your mind?"

"Your four children."

The front door banged open and in they charged from the playscape.

"Larry grabbed my swing," Jenny sobbed.

"Ray's hogging the slide," Danny cried.

"That's why I need to get out of the house. Don't you think I deserve a break?"

"No! Your first responsibility is to your children. When Mr. Borsuk offered me a job at his pharmacy around the corner, "I said, 'No. I have to take care of my two children.'"

I look at Mom, her skin smooth, her brown hair in a pixie, still a beauty. But after her Holocaust losses, she had to make sure we were safe. How could I argue?

Mom barely escaped from Nazi Europe. I grew up protecting her. Always the good girl, never contradicting.

When my college boyfriend said, "I don't know anyone your age who insists their mother is always right," I said, "Well, mine is."

I believed it until three years later, when I was about to marry Stu—the cute nerd I had met at Harvard—and Mom insisted that, instead of setting up our own apartment, we move in and share my bedroom in my parents' Bronx apartment.

"If not for Hitler, I never would have left my parents."

"But this is America, 1965, not Zurawno."

I was picturing making love everywhere in our own apartment, alone at last! No way would I give up our privacy, not even for Mom. Stu was relieved.

To prepare for my escape from full-time mothering, I became a doctoral student. A few years later, after auditing two creative writing courses, I began writing family stories. I gave Mom the manuscript of my first chapbook to read and told her to share it with her cousin, Celia, a retired high school English teacher. Her only response: "Celia said you can't write, you're wasting your time."

It's a shame Mom didn't read it, or she would've realized that I'd internalized her Zurawno stories, that she was my muse. Again, she said nothing when, a year later, I gave her my first chapbook, published by a local press. But she didn't stop trying to discourage me.

"My dentist said, 'Writing is a black hole.'"

"What do you expect him to say? All he sees are black holes."

How quickly the years passed. Finally, when the kids were away at college and graduate school, my dream opportunity arrived. During

Stu's sabbaticals at L'université de Grenoble, I sometimes taught an elective. After teaching the first creative writing class, I accepted a full-time position.

Stu understood that, after my years of putting family first, nothing was negotiable.

Mom tried her best to discourage me. First, she tried manipulation: "Your mother-in-law is very unhappy with you."

When that didn't work, she asked, "Aren't you afraid Stuie will find another woman?"

"He could find one when I'm home," I assured her. "Stop worrying about me; I'm fifty years old."

"You'll see. Your children will always be your children," Mom said in her unwavering, eighty-two-year-old voice.

About that, she was right. But I've learned from Mom not to impose my opinions on my children. Only when asked do I offer. Otherwise, I try to keep quiet. I raised them to be responsible, capable, independent adults. Besides, it's a full-time job just living my life.

Close Encounter of the Episcopal Kind

by ANGELA BONAVOGLIA

It's Easter Sunday 1985. I always try to go to Mass with my mother on Easter Sunday, either in my hometown, Scranton, or my new town, Brooklyn. But this year my faith is in shambles. Not my faith in God, but my faith in the institution and the men who run it. Despite how angry I am about the Catholic Church's miserable treatment of women, I can't let go. My mother shares my ambivalence. But she's adamant: "Don't let them keep you away," she says.

This Easter, again, I won't. But this Easter will be different. This Easter, I decide, I will take a public stand.

I have no idea what that stand will be.

My mother and I settle into a back pew at St. Peter's Cathedral for the eleven o'clock Easter High Mass—that would be the ceremonial extravaganza, very long and very crowded. Down the aisle come the altar boys, young, scrubbed, aglow; Monsignor, decked out in his finery; local priests, all male; and finally, the bishop, elaborate miter on his head, gold crozier in his hand, resplendent in shimmering white and gold vestments.

The bishop begins to celebrate Mass, leading us all in prayer. Eventually it comes time for Communion. "With this bread, I give you my body," he says. "With this wine, I give you my blood." They are Jesus's words, the gift of self in its most elemental form.

Then begins the voiceless journey of the people, moving forward to the Communion rail. No one speaks at the Communion rail except the priest, to say in reverence, "Body of Christ," and the communicant to say, "Amen." Speaking there is absolutely verboten.

I join the Communion line. I know I'm playing with fire. I know the rules: no confession, no Communion. I've not been to confession or Communion since I was twenty-four. That's when a lecherous old priest invited me out of the confessional into his parlor to drool over me—when I walked out, leaving him and the idea of priests as little gods behind. Still, in the eyes of the churchmen, I have no business on this line.

As I take small steps forward, I make another decision, a radical decision. I will speak at the Communion rail.

Palms sweating, heart pounding, I am soon standing before the bishop. The line stops moving behind me. The altar boys flanking the bishop look on in horrified anticipation.

Out of my mouth comes a simple statement: "Father, you have a long way to go to make women equal in this Church."

The bishop freezes, holding the chalice in one hand and in the other, the Host, my Host, in midair.

I stand there, staring, immovable.

The bishop needs to get me out of the way. "Are you taking communion?" he asks.

Without hesitation, I hear myself reply, "Yes."

"Have you been to confession?" he asks, unmistakable indictment in his voice.

Guilt rises up in me for a moment, but only for a moment. "Yes," I say, because I have, in my own way.

I take Communion.

"We can talk about this," he says quietly as I leave. "This just isn't the time or the place."

The next day, I call the rectory to request an audience with the bishop.

He's friendly. We sit face-to-face. I argue for women priests. I tell him that one day, he and the other churchmen will have to account to

God for closing women out of the Church the way they have. I tell him he should see *Yentl*. He's never heard of *Yentl*. It's Barbra Streisand's directorial debut where she stars as a deeply devout, ingenious Jewish girl who longs to study the Torah, which is forbidden to women, and finds a way to do it. I love that film.

The bishop wants to know about me. I tell him I work for Planned Parenthood. I expect a reaction. Nothing. I decide to provoke.

"Are you going to excommunicate me?" I ask.

"Well, you don't publicly advocate for abortion," he says, thinking he's rescuing me.

"I'm pro-choice," I assert, "like Planned Parenthood." That's advocacy enough, I think.

I don't expect him to threaten excommunication. He doesn't.

Amicably, we part ways. As I leave, he probably thinks I'm still in the flock. In fact, I am one with all the other Fallen Women. We are, all of us, in a forest of kindling, waiting to catch fire.

Life Alert

by KRYSIA CARMEL NELSON

"Help! I've fallen and I can't get up!" The iconic tagline for Life Alert pops into my head as I watch the nurse unplug the machines monitoring my father's now lifeless body. He fell and broke his neck, and a Life Alert monitor would not have saved him. Now he is gone, unexpectedly freed from a dysfunctional body ravaged by age and injury. I look at you, standing there beside me, and am stunned by a sense of envy at my father's newfound freedom. Trapped by the horror that our marriage has become, divorcing you seems like a fitting final homage to my father. From the great beyond, he would be thrilled at the prospect and simultaneously furious that he did not live to see the day.

I used to adore you. Once upon a time, I felt we were soulmates with a shared commitment to a dream that included building a family and a life and growing old together in sickness and in health. But the day you got fired from your dream job, the anger, the depression, and the drinking came to define your entire being. You never rebounded. You became completely dysfunctional, and the stint in rehab was a sham. It was no longer about us; it became about you—seduced by vodka, in a sickness whose recovery only you can realize.

You are a mean drunk. For at least seven years I have begged you to get sober. When I staged an intervention during a couple's therapy session and the shrink commented that I might not like you sober, I did not expect he would be right. You have not gotten sober, but I have discovered that in your rare sober moments, I do not like you any more than when you are drunk.

You insist that you love me, but I found your handwritten list of things you hate about me. If written words mean anything, your spoken professions of love are a lie. But it turns out, with you, it is all a lie. Stone cold sober, you steal from us, perpetuating a pattern of high crimes and misdemeanors that predates our wedding. Did you think I would not notice? I notice everything. That's why I found the condom in the pocket of the pants you were wearing when you came home at 1:00 a.m. You got drunk on Mother's Day and called me a bitch no fewer than ten times in the span of an hour. A week later, stone cold sober, you handed me a $50 bill and told me to go buy myself the chocolates you thought about giving me but did not. These are not hallmarks of love.

Perhaps worse than the lies and the theft and the hatefulness is the lack of remorse. You never apologize for anything—not for the sloppy inebriation, not for the gratuitous profanity, not for the hurtful digs, not for letting us down, not for stealing, not for lying, not for ruining every holiday and special occasion for more than a decade.

I used to joke that I was the trophy wife. The joke was on me, not set on the mantel like a prize but mounted above it like prey. You have shown me who you are. I have seen enough.

I have asked myself why I stay. But as the Green Day song lyrics go, "why" is not a question but a lesson learned in time. All these years I have waited for you to be a reliable life partner. But you failed me. "Until death do us part" was the deal, and now, here we are—figuratively, finally.

I feel a lightness as I pack, and relief that I will be freed from the daily stress of not knowing exactly what harsh words or thoughtless acts my psyche will have to endure. But the next moment, I feel overwhelming sadness that the story of our lives will not end the way we had written it more than two decades ago. I realize I must mourn not the end of our marriage but the loss of the dream I had for my life as your wife.

The key fob for the car is in my hand, an array of buttons available for the pressing. Which function to choose? Lock? Unlock? Panic? Ignition start? I finger it in my palm. *I got this.*

I will rise up on my own now, thanks.

Green Beans

by MONIQUE HELLER

My mom obeyed two people—God and my dad.

I did not. I was the unintended and unplanned third daughter, born just shy of eleven months following my middle sister's entrance into the world. Irish twins they called us, despite not a drop of Irish blood among us. I spoiled their vision of the nuclear family—2.2 kids did not mean three.

When I learned about the birds and the bees, I did the amateur calculation in my head and realized that my mother's OB-GYN had probably just issued her the "green light" to commence marital relations when I was conceived. Questioning my dad, I asked him how he could have been so "needy." He snorted, "What makes you think it was me?"

Ewwwww! It COULDN'T have been my mom! She wasn't the horny one in the relationship, was she?

Poor Mom. Religious to a fault, she believed that God would only give her what she could handle. The guilt of taking birth control and preventing a life outweighed her capacity for reason. The toll and exhaustion of bearing three babies in three years wore heavily on her until the point of what we later called her "nervous breakdown." I was blamed for that—as well as her hemorrhoids and varicose veins. My dad and the Church eventually parted ways. He never set foot in another one, even after he died.

It was tough for me. How does one differentiate themselves when they have older sisters who have worn the same homemade clothes that became your patched-up, too-small, high-waisted (I got the height in the family) hand-me-downs and had the same teachers you had, and who heard ad nauseum about them from everybody every—and I mean EVERY—day?

I made myself distinct. Early on I learned that if I put up enough of a fuss, my mom, avoiding conflict, would cater to my whims and make me a "special" dish. She was Italian, and therefore onions, tomatoes, and peppers appeared on every plate. I hated them. Every single one of them. Were they in a dish? Nope. Wouldn't eat it. In a salad? Nope. Wouldn't pick around them.

Then came the night when my dad decided he'd had enough of my finicky ways. He slapped some green beans on my plate. These were not the fresh, bright-green crisp beans from a garden, but the canned version. Limp, lifeless pale versions of their former selves, these grotesque items demanded to be served with a slotted spoon to "drain the juices."

Oh, hell no, my ten-year-old self secretly thought.

I didn't sign up for them, and I didn't put them on my plate. I was not going be part of the "Clean Plate Club."

I sat there, alternately staring at the beans and glaring at my dad, planning the demise of one of them.

I sat at the table for hours until I was excused and went to bed hungry.

Like a waking nightmare, the beans showed up for breakfast the very next morning. By this time, they were cold and had begun their descent into a stringy pile of mush. *Hell to the no*, I swore silently. My father had been a sailor, and his vivid vocabulary had been transmitted to me, whether he knew it or not.

The beans were packed for my school lunch in a chilled thermos lest they come to room temperature.

A smarter kid would have thrown them out at lunch, then lied and said they ate them. Was I smart enough to do that? Definitely not. I brought those slimy bastards back home with me. Whammo! They were on the dinner plate again.

At this point, my mother was in despair. "Joseph, she hasn't eaten in over a day!"

My father told me I had the choice of eating them or the wooden spoon. I chose the latter. As I was walking down the hallway to my cramped bedroom awaiting my fate, I whispered under my breath but loudly enough for him to hear, "I told you that I wasn't eating those fucking beans."

I felt powerful and liberated. I was and am certain that I was the only woman who had EVER talked to him like that—a little girl's voice speaking in his own language and using his own tone.

From that time forward, we had an understanding about each other's mettle. I learned I could make my own choices. And he knew he had met his match.

Worth My Salt

by ERICA BUEHLER

In the last twelve months, I have eaten remarkable things. I've tasted the highest quality Wagyu beef sliced into the five smallest pieces of meat I have ever called a dinner. I have cracked open the legs of seasonal, exclusively West Coast lobster arriving at $62 per pound. I've had hand-pinched pastas so delicate they melted in my mouth, and everything was accompanied by some puréed cauliflower or immaculate reduction or gold flecks and a kiss from God.

The best part? The meals were free; taken care of by a PR firm here or a representative there, all in hopes that I would wield my power of words to generate buzz about whichever restaurant I was sampling, which I did.

Except, nearly every time, whether alone, with a friend, or whoever was lucky enough to come with me, I felt the same surge of panic and fear run through me as I prayed to the lords of finance and bank accounts that I had enough money to cover an adequate tip.

The thing is, I was never terribly different from the folks bringing over the dishes. In fact, I envied their consistent streams of income, their generous tips, and felt sympathy for the struggles brought upon their work by the pandemic. Still, I would tip them, leave my business card, and make a courteous exit, speed-running to my car as if that would save me a few cents on my parking garage ticket. During the weeks when I had not committed to such meals, I was at home eating boxed mac and cheese and single-serving ramen.

I like to call this phenomenon the "Irony of the Broke Food Writer," because whenever someone asks me what I do and I tell them, their eyes flicker with delight and intrigue. "That's so cool!" "I bet you've been to a lot of restaurants." "Do you get to eat for free?" And I'll politely answer their questions while holding back the urge to shout, "This is, actually, how I'm avoiding hunger. I'm kind of a giant fraud."

I don't *really* think I'm a fraud, though I've certainly written some clickbaity content in my time. *Did you see what this celebrity chef posted on Instagram?* I'm proud of many of the clips I have published. But for today's importance of writers and journalists and media people—whether that's relaying the news or keeping companies afloat—we sure don't get paid our worth.

And so, when I essentially had to pivot to full-time freelancing as a green twenty-five-year-old who'd barely scratched the surface of the publishing world (I got a *lot* of surprised looks), it was about doing the work and stretching my experiences further than I thought they would go. This meant pitching and legwork and carpooling to restaurants and only finishing half the meal so I could take a to-go box and have lunch for the next day. It meant arriving twenty minutes early and endlessly circling the block so I didn't have to pay for parking. It meant doing digital acrobatics, transferring whichever meager funds I could gather into a single account, then bracing for the overdraft fee.

So, what? Is the point of this to reiterate "Don't judge a book by its cover?" Maybe. But it's more a word to the wise for folks who constantly feel like what they're doing isn't enough—who are relentlessly plagued by imposter syndrome. Here's the secret: Everyone's an imposter, and no one is. There isn't a single person on this planet who always knows the plan and how to execute it perfectly; we're all just doing what we can to make it to the next day (while praying that the next will be better than today). If we take the humble, lowly jobs or play bank-account Tetris in order to get a hot meal, so be it.

I once had a mentor tell me that you have to do the grunt work before you get to the good stuff. But the good stuff *does* come, as long as you're willing to persevere—to really get your hands dirty, get hurt, and fail. To, in other words, fall—and to rise. Often. Repeatedly. And

I think, even if I could grab my younger self by the shoulders and shout all of this at her, that it just wouldn't resonate the way it does once you've lived through the hardship.

I want to tell her we'll come out smiling, always more self-assured on the other side and, usually, surprisingly, satisfied.

Moving Out; Moving In

by CINDY EASTMAN

I walked up the stairs to the apartment, clutching the keys in my hand so tightly I created small red ridges in my fingers, as if releasing them might make my new home disappear. My Volvo wagon was packed to the moonroof in the driveway, but I had no desire to start hauling my meager possessions up to the second floor—yet. I had only found the place a few days earlier, briefly spending minutes inside before rushing back to the real estate office to sign the lease. It hadn't mattered what it looked like—it was affordable and vacant, my top two criteria. As I opened the door and walked into the empty kitchen, I felt a strange sensation inside my chest. It was relief.

The apartment was an oddly laid out rental above a dentist's office in a Colonial on Main Street. It could work. Advertised as a two-bedroom, I needed three and fashioned one out of a curious little space off the living room for my six-year-old son. (He'd fit.) My twelve-year-old daughter would get the normal-size bedroom and I'd take the smaller room off the kitchen. It *would* work. Five-foot-high cherry-stained windows encircled the main dining/living room, but the house was surrounded by trees, so there was a semblance of privacy. Industrial-grade blue carpeting covered the uneven floors except in the kitchen, which was a beige linoleum. We would be one big happy, new family in our second-floor aerie above the town green, now that I had moved us out of our home and away from my marriage.

I had quietly packed up the car that morning so as not to disturb sleepy girls just waking up after my daughter's birthday slumber party, looking for doughnuts and juice. I still cringe at my timing, but I was driven by the urgent desire to get out after having spent the previous eight months living in the dramatic, tragic collapse of a relationship. My husband thought I wouldn't do it—which gave me the window of opportunity to get away. I took as many of my personal belongings as I could stuff in the car, believing I would never be allowed back in the house once I left. (I was right.)

I went down and wrestled the coffeemaker and my one bag of groceries from the back seat of the car and went upstairs. Once the coffee was brewing and I had stowed a couple of essentials in the fridge, I started opening cupboards and drawers as if some magic would provide me with what I would need to make this work. But they were empty. Just like all the closets, shelves, and cabinets in every other room. I went back into the kitchen, painted a pleasant light pink and more like a kitchenette, but with enough room to fit a table for three. Too bad I hadn't managed to cram such a thing into the car.

I poured coffee in my favorite mug and walked with it into the living room and sat down cross-legged against the wall under one of those five-foot windows. That strange sensation of relief returned, and this time it was accompanied by another sensation: I was smiling. I was enveloped by an almost sensual sense of well-being, and I knew at that moment I had made the right decision. All the pain of what had been and all the fear of what was to come had brought me to this; sitting on the floor of my new home, I was right where I was supposed to be.

Over the years, I've relived this day through different images in my mind: the cold, gray January weather, bare windows looking out on the trees—black branches against a stark winter sky. Fragrant coffee brewing on the counter. My empty bedroom that wouldn't even contain a bed until almost a month later. All the challenges I had anticipated in planning my escape were nothing compared to the actual ordeals I ended up facing. The town in Shirley Jackson's "The Lottery" looked friendly compared to my town when I decided to disrupt the status quo by leaving my husband. The eventual divorce was acrimonious; our friends took a side—his. My apartment in the treetops became my sanctuary. But the strongest memory, what is still as clear to me now as that first morning, is that sense of relief that told me I could do it. Turns out, I could.

Put Out to Pasture

By DANA STARR

I wasn't frisked or handcuffed. No tempers flared. No voices raised. No accusations leveled or denied. I'd done nothing wrong according to the two men who flanked me in the long hallway. Their words had the ring of truth but the sting of a lie.

We passed cubicles; people averted their gazes. I was grateful not to see pity or surprise or glee in their eyes. None of them, including the men escorting me, would be there but for the work I'd done years earlier. I'd been part of a small team hired to get a large energy company up and running in the middle of nowhere.

I saw the cardboard box at the end of the hallway in front of my very own cubicle. The Human Resources representative on my left informed me that I had twenty minutes, per company policy, to pack my belongings and leave. The supervisor on my right offered to bring more boxes if I needed them. At least I think that's what he said. I noticed a faint thudding.

I collapsed in the office chair I'd complained about for almost seven years. I wasn't going to miss that chair. I was going to miss the money, excellent benefits, and even more excellent friends I'd made on the job. A picture of some of them, wearing company T-shirts I'd designed, hung in front of me. They were eating hot dogs in celebration of a stellar safety record under a tent on the massive construction site. That was one of the many events—large to small, formal to casual, expensive to cheap—I had coordinated at the company. The thudding was not going away.

I took the picture off the wall and placed it in a box that had previously held thirty-six rolls of toilet paper, according to the illustration on the side. I placed the plaque I'd received for being the United Way campaign chairperson next to the picture, followed by a framed certificate acknowledging my service as Rotary Club president. There was plenty of room left in the box for the Above and Beyond award I'd received from the company. I stared at it, wondering how I'd gone from above and beyond to laid-off. The thudding was rhythmic and powerful.

I had four drawers to empty. Rummaging through stray paper clips, a broken stapler, and a three-hole punch, I found a stash of tote bags from various conferences, workshops, and seminars. Not one of those events had prepared me for what to do next. What do you do when the thing you do, the thing you are good at, the thing you've done to the distraction and detriment of most everything else in your life, including your own family, ceases to exist? The thudding was deafening.

I threw the tote bags and broken stapler in the trash. On a whim, I tossed the three-hole punch in the toilet paper box. Technically, it didn't belong to me. Technically, I didn't give a damn. If I couldn't have my job, my sense of self, my reason for being, at least I could have a three-hole punch.

The thudding slowed and finally stopped. The source of the sound was with me, in me. It was the high horse I'd fallen from. She'd galloped to my side, loyal as ever. We'd had quite the ride.

She'd never missed any of my speaking engagements on behalf of the company. It didn't matter if it was an early-morning breakfast meeting of the chamber of commerce or a late night of drinks and dinner at the country club with legislative members of Congress. I could always count on her to be there for me.

She was with me on every first-class trip to the company headquarters in Europe. We particularly enjoyed the warm towels provided after eating hot fudge sundaes over the Atlantic Ocean.

No more towels, tote bags, or trips. Together, we'd been put out to pasture. That was the truth no matter how much I wanted it to be a lie, and it did sting. It still does for that matter, but I've worked hard to not let it define me or make me bitter. I'm worth more than that—a lot more than that.

Holding back tears, her by my side, I picked up the toilet paper box and walked out of the building to face an uncertain future with my head held high. At least I had good memories, a 401(k), and a three-hole punch.

Taking It Off

by ANGEL JOHNSTONE

My stockbroker's license had not prepared me for being broke. It had not prepared me for business expenses or debt or bankruptcy. It hadn't prepared me at all for the bumpy road to success.

I was alone. No significant other. No parental help. I had no regular job to answer to, just a failing business and a last-ditch chance to make it work. I didn't ask anyone what they thought. I just called the ad. I set up the audition.

Two days and many mental gymnastics later, I arrived at a seedy office building. His office stank of stale cigars, and the couch gave off casting director vibes. I steadied my nerves, talked it all over, got my instructions, and wiggled my best to the music. Whole thing might have taken twenty minutes from the time I parked. I got the gig. An address, a name, and a "good luck" sealed the deal. I had become an exotic dancer.

Taking your clothes off for money is hard. It is hard on your legs and on feet crammed into stiletto heels. It is hard on your knees as you pick up the dollars from the floor. It is hard on your sense of self-worth as you float around, selling a private encounter that feels intimate but can be the furthest thing from it. It is hard on your self-image as you compare yourself to the beauties in the room. Ultimately, it is hard to know that you have fallen this far, this fast.

It is also liberating: an awakening and catharsis all in one. You get to pick a new name, a new wardrobe, and an entirely new persona. You can choose to be the version of yourself that you have never given license to occupy you before. You can try, test, and literally trip over yourself as you figure yourself out. There are few expectations and fewer requirements. The bar is so low, it got tipped and turned into a pole.

You have pitched yourself headlong off the "good girl" pedestal to find yourself center stage in the "bad girl" mystique. Congratulations! You will never judge yourself against the same standards again.

Money flows.

Music flows around you.

Your body becomes more fluid, toned and graceful.

Your ears keener to the conversations nearby.

Your eyes more accustomed to the dark and to the look of desire.

You learn how to use eye contact as a magnet and your movement as a motivator.

You find your boundaries and decide when to bend them.

You often find sisterhood and laughter.

You sometimes hear compelling stories of grief and redemption.

You rarely go thirsty.

You never have to go home alone.

You almost always will.

To have "fallen" young was a gift I never knew I had opened until I got older.

I regained my footing in my career and climbed the corporate ladder, but I always had this secret other version of myself that hung out in the recesses of my mind. I felt different from other women. I felt more embodied and sexually aware than my contemporary female friends. When feeling disempowered, I had a persona to back my confidence up. I didn't know until decades later how unusual that was.

Years later, when I started to honestly talk with women about their life experiences, it became clear that my conditioning as a "good" girl had been greatly diminished in those years. When wearing nothing but a thong at work had become normal, I had gotten comfortable with me. I simply didn't feel as guilty about my body as these women did.

I was far more sexually active and enjoying it more than the women I knew. I didn't have the same level of shame attached to my activities.

One of the best aspects of falling off the pedestal early is that you get around to the business of being who you are so much faster.

I am learning to embrace my fallen women status as an aging crone. I am throwing caution to the wind and publishing my erotica stories. I am finding my voice and amplifying it as a drumbeat for women to give up their good girl persona for their inner vixen earlier and more often.

I am doing the scary thing of naming my desires and showing up to receive them.

This alone is radical.

It is an act of social defiance and brazen recklessness. It is high time we all take the fall.

I Fell Fast for My Baby Girl

by CRISTINA CABRAL CARUK

I was a sleep-deprived, mentally and physically exhausted mother and lawyer.

In the first couple of months of my infant's life, every sound the baby made I interpreted. I used a tape recorder to chronicle the moans and gasps for air so I could show my "evidence" to the pediatrician.

When I returned to full-time work, I vowed to come home every lunch hour to nurse my daughter. The office was two miles from my home in Wethersfield.

My boss asked me to try a case for him in New Britain when my child was about four months. It involved a pedestrian struck by a car. I was excited and nervous at the same time. I had never tried a jury case before. Only bench trials. I called my husband from the courthouse during a recess from jury selection. I broke down, sobbing uncontrollably, and could not hang up. I longed to hold and nurse my baby. I was her mama and she needed me. I composed myself and dried my tears before I returned to the courtroom.

That case was settled after two days of jury selection. It wasn't the only matter that settled. That experience made me realize I did not want to be a trial lawyer as a new mama. Too many demands. No flexibility. I knew I could be a better lawyer if I was not a mom, and I could excel in motherhood if I gave up law. It did not matter that my boss had just rewarded me with a raise.

Nevertheless, I resigned from my full-time job. I was not sleeping or eating well, and it did not make any sense. My father was furious when he heard I had left a job without having a new one.

I was a shell of the person I had been prior. I contemplated walking in front of a moving car. This reminded me of the jury case I handled before my abrupt departure from lawyering. I was bound up in a knot of anxiety and stress. I felt like a snake was coiling itself around my throat and barred me from speaking my truth.

My father insisted that I had lost my mind.

I was treated by a doctor, sought therapy, and fell to my knees in prayer.

In therapy, I questioned everything I knew about myself. Did I actually graduate from law school? Did I pass the bar? I recalled my doctor ironically recording me just as I had recorded my daughter. He asked me a barrage of questions, including where I went to school and why my husband didn't work.

Once I was on medication, my anxiety shrunk like a wool sweater in a dryer. I was ready to work again.

Squeezing myself into a navy-blue pinstriped skirt, I tucked in my crisp white pleated blouse and then slipped into the matching blazer. I placed the baby in the carrier. She was fussing and wanted a bottle. I glanced at my watch and saw I had time to feed her before the meeting at the Law Registry.

The representative at the registry was blonde, slim, and statuesque. When I walked in lugging the travel carrier with my infant, she seemed surprised. During the meeting, she asked me background questions to determine which interview she would send me on, and the child visibly distracted her. She repeatedly tried to make the baby smile at her. "I don't know why she is not smiling. All the babies I ever meet smile at me." I explained that she was tired and usually napped at that hour. At the end of our conversation, the lady provided me with the details of a position that highly appealed to me, and the baby smiled

146

at her. It would be a four-month assignment covering the maternity leave of a staff counsel for a leading insurer.

The following week I interviewed for the position. I would be covering for a former classmate, who I recognized immediately upon entering the interview room. The meeting ran swimmingly well. I did not take my baby to this particular appointment, as I was able to secure a sitter.

I received the offer the next day. A twenty-five-hour workweek and generous hourly wage.

I no longer felt trapped like a battle-tested prisoner-at-law.

Lost and Found

by PAT PANNELL

She isn't thrilled about slogging into the city. After all, the day's mandatory turkey won't stuff itself. Nevertheless, she resolves to do it all. Rising early, she gathers juice boxes and snacks to be pulverized in backpacks by midmorning, old coloring books and broken crayons for the tedious train ride, hats and mismatched gloves preapproved for loss, mini-Kleenex for mini-noses. She assigns clothing, slings breakfast, and musters the troops—one spouse, two daughters, one friend and neighbor with second-grade child in tow. She hurries the group through Penn Station and forges north, joining the festive ribbon of humanity lining Central Park West on this icy bright November morning. Making memories!

She's scouting an ideal "watch spot" when the masses ahead suddenly part like a metropolitan Red Sea, generously offering up-front seats to their trio of little ones for an unobstructed view of floats and balloons. The parents, always overprotective but particularly wary in this urban landscape, initially hesitate—but then relent. Although several rows of adults will be separating the girls from perfect hands-on supervision, they'll be right against the barricades, seemingly trapped in place. Their tiny heads remain intermittently visible through the thicket of full-grown arms and legs, their tiny bottoms glued to the curb.

Until one is not—that of the youngest, just three. One minute nestled snugly against her sister of six, the next: disappeared. The second-grader shouts back that the smallest is no longer with them. They assure her she's mistaken—look again, harder. Her response is insistent, frantic: "She's NOT HERE!" And before the sentence is

148

even completed, they are bulldozing forward, scanning, searching for flowered jeans and pink puff jacket. Vanished.

Once the mother accepts this as undeniable fact, her world begins spinning. The looming skyscrapers, surrounding throng, ground beneath; all are in motion. Every inch of her skin burns with pins-and-needles heat as the floor drops from her stomach. Her child could be anywhere—in any of those high-rises, down any of those streets. How far could she have gotten—been taken—in the time that has elapsed, is elapsing even now?

Is she gone?

This impossible possible fells her. Knees buckling, vision blacking, she crumples—until her husband catches her and she abruptly snaps to, noting everything in ultrasharp focus. A panicked voice is yelling, describing the missing, and she realizes it's her own voice, but hoarse, unfamiliar.

People turn, murmur, stare. Within two minutes, spanning two eternities, a stranger appears to say a child has been found nearby, jostled, disoriented, crying "Mommy." Scooped up and handed to police, she's been taken ten blocks south for "holding." Another onlooker stops a young officer, who radios to confirm the girl's whereabouts and then asks the wild-eyed mother to wait while he goes to check.

WAIT?!?!

Bystanders object before she even finds words. "You CRAZY?!" "No way! TAKE her!" Facing mounting pressure, the chastened rookie caves.

Which is how she joins the Macy's parade, dazed, half-jogging between a Midwestern marching band and a formation of handlers who wrangle a gigantic cat inflatable above. Blown down the wide avenue, unable to sense pavement underfoot or distinguish faces flashing by, she feels teleported—traversing a surreal universe of blurred color and distorted sound on her way to the "Lost and Found Zone."

And then she is there.

Her terrified, sobbing baby, secured in another's arms but, upon catching sight of her mother, thrashing to launch herself to the one whose job it is to protect her, always—the one who has failed. In less than a heart's beat, the space between them collapses. Absolution. There is no end then of shushing, kissing, squeezing, more kissing, the promise of infinite kisses. The only proof that they actually belong to each other, kisses.

Quickly now, reversing the route just taken, they set off to rejoin guilt-ridden father, traumatized sister, distraught companions, all left agonizing in place. Cradling a curled-up bundle that somehow has fallen asleep amid the chaos, the mother race-walks, this time against the marchers, skirting their perimeter. She begins to calm, finally able to breathe and register the crowd of cordoned-off spectators alongside, clapping, calling out, "You found her!" "HOORAY!" and "Happy Holidays!"

She recognizes them—smiling, cheering angels of every size and shape—and gives thanks.

Letter to My Eighteen-Year-Old Self

by SUSAN COSSETTE

Hey, Blondie,

put away that strawberry Bonne Bell lip gloss. Yeah, you. I come from the future, with a serious conversation.

Turn down the damned Van Halen. Sit down on the orange-plush chair in Mama's living room; dig your red-polished toes deep into the green shag carpet and pay attention. Oh, and put out that menthol cigarette. You will get asthma and quit in twenty years, but your future self is having a hard time breathing right now.

Anyway, here goes.

Do not be embarrassed by the little pink house you grew up in. Don't be ashamed that your father wore crazy plaid polyester trousers (it was the 1970s, after all) instead of a blue blazer and khakis and that he wasn't some stiff-lipped titan of industry. He was a TV repairman, and you got the first edition of *Pong* for free in 1974. The old Ford Galaxy 500 in the driveway is now a collector's dream, and that tiny house is worth more than $500,000 now, or so says Zillow.

Don't listen to your mother and take that corporate job just because it offers health insurance and a retirement plan. You will end up a misfit, although you may be grateful later for the pension. But still. And whatever you do, do NOT let anyone tell you that a blouse with a foulard bow tie is appealing on any occasion. Reject blue pinstripe suits, and those Ferragamo pumps with the little grosgrain bows. Don't ignore me.

Stay in grad school. Write. Take that teaching job at King School that Mrs. Cesare offered you in 1993, even if it was only half-time. It's all right to be a little broke in your twenties.

You will marry up in life—not that poet's son, but the doctor's son from Darien. Just don't do either, at least not when you're twenty-three. Maybe don't do it at all, ever.

You will have a child; that part *was* right. He was the best thing you ever made, finer and stronger than any poem and more enduring than the paper you wrote on *Orlando* in 1992, or your thesis on Plath and Dickinson.

You will have an affair. Two of them, if you must know. Yes, I see you smirking. I am not surprising you. You will dance barefoot in the streets of New Orleans singing "Bye Bye Miss American Pie," waltzing with a grown man dressed in a diaper. Seriously, you will.

You will leave home with three suitcases and the fat orange cat in his carrier. You will think about what happened after you closed that door for the last time, the Hedda Gabler slam heard round the world, or at least throughout Darien.

What did your family say to one another afterward? Did they go about the morning as if nothing had happened, or did they stare blankly at the rhododendrons and listen to the traffic rustling by on Noroton Avenue as the world carried on? You will never know, but their faces will haunt you. That's all right.

You will never be allowed into the home you created and then destroyed. Three girl cats still wait on the bed for you. Your mother's lily-of-the-valley dishes still remain in the cabinets, and all your report cards are in a plastic bin in the garage, growing mold alongside fading Polaroids from 1968.

You left on your own, but they will always say you fell. Lady Daedalus, girl, your wax wings held up.

Hey, the next time we meet, you will have become a redhead—plump and surly and writing letters to your past self and worrying about your cancer surgery in nineteen days. You're going to be all right. There will just be a little scar.

And now until we meet again, *adios, au revoir*; don't you behave.

Good night.

Old Friends

by MELISSA BABCOCK JOHNSON

After two years at an all-girls' high school, I swapped skirts and nuns for jeans and boys and returned to public education in the fall of 1999.

While I had loved the lack of jerks with bowl cuts hurling dodgeballs at me in gym class, being around boys again was a thrill, even though the ones in my small town might as well have been my cousins. I'd watched them cry in kindergarten, wet their Bugle Boy jeans in first grade, pick their noses in second, and puke in third.

In fourth grade, a few of those boys learned I had been stung on the playground. One exclaimed he couldn't "believe a bee would sting someone so ugly!" Boys would fling that word my way often over the following years. Never mind that I was tall and thin with green eyes, clear skin, and a nose people pay for. Curly hair and glasses? Ugly.

I'd left the boys at thirteen. Now we were sixteen. I guess I'd undergone a transformation (see: glow up) during my hiatus, despite the Sisters trying to keep me humble. Skirts to the knees, ladies. We're here to learn, not to look pretty. And learn what? English, math, science, art, but also—girls racing out of religion class crying because they were headed to hell for fooling around with boys. Or for wanting to fool around with boys. Or girls.

Safe in my heathen high school, I ditched my bifocals and brushed the knots out of my hair. No one would mistake me for Britney Spears, but that and some Maybelline were enough to render me pretty.

I fell in with a group of guys, none of whom had lived in town before seventh grade. They called me Babs, a nod to my last name. The five of us had Desktop Publishing together and often spent the class period seeing who could make the funniest clip art sign. Their crushes on me waxed and waned. (See: proximity infatuation.) I pretended not to care but relished the attention. No one was calling me ugly now—I would even be voted "changed the most" senior year.

Male friendships were simple and refreshing. Other girls were fun and offered a kinship boys couldn't, but some brought drama and required mind reading. If I argued with one of the guys, he'd ask if I was on my period, I'd punch him in the arm, and we'd move on. Offend a fellow teenage girl? She might tell you at the ten-year reunion after a few drinks.

Two of the guys and I attended the same university. I dated one, but we had left a school of two hundred girls for one with ten thousand women. He fell for a busty blonde art major, and we were history before Valentine's Day. The girl next door replaced by the girl next dorm. (See: market saturation.)

My latest transformation was longer and less flattering. I got breast cancer in 2015 and focused on being alive instead of being desired. That adventure also resulted in my choosing not to have children. What a waste of a womb! (See: sarcasm.)

I've gained seventy-three pounds since the principal handed me my diploma. I recently made myself platinum blonde but destroyed my hair and had to shave my head, bringing back my chemo-chic look. Which for me looks like the Michelin Man headbutted a porcupine. If I wear a flannel shirt and pass a mirror, for a second I think that a trucker named Melvin broke into my house.

Today, the guys and I are staring forty in the un-Botoxed face. We meet in the group chat instead of the hallway. Rather than letting me copy their math homework, they advise me on my 401(k). They've invited me to gatherings, but part of me didn't believe I'd matter to them now. If I'm a female who breaks the Laws of Attraction (Who the hell legislates those, anyway? Maybelline?), what good am I? But one of the guys recently told me, "one hundred pounds or three hundred pounds, you're still Babs." Their friend.

The lithe sixteen-year-old with long hair is long gone, forever frozen in the yearbook pages. I want to tell her that being easy on the eyes might make her life a bit easier, but it doesn't do much for anyone else. And when she's forty, here's what she'll be good for: friendship, generosity, humor, support, and understanding. If you look closely, you'll see the same sparkle in her eyes. Beautiful the whole time.

The Iron and the Belt

by KIM A. HANSON

For most people, Saturday mornings are a day of rest and relief, a day of ease.

At the age of thirteen my Saturday mornings were spent in drudgery, a pile of ironing my misery.

As the oldest daughter in a first-generation Italian-American family, I was being held captive to a process my parents called "my education into womanhood." This education included learning to avoid actions attributed to bad girls (or *putana*) who wore too-short skirts and stayed out late with boys—and undertaking so-called "good wife" actions by practicing the skills needed for effective housework and, inherently, efficient servitude to the two men in our household.

I was given a hot iron, a spray bottle of water, and piles of my father's cotton shirts and my brother's blue jeans to work through. In those days, jeans were not the soft friendly fabric we now all know and love. They were stiff, unyielding pieces of tough fabric that you had to truly press to have a prayer of getting the wrinkles out.

As I labored, my mother gossiped on the phone, connected by a long, mustard-yellow phone cord, which allowed her to be in the kitchen supervising me and then around the corner into the living room, swapping stories with her friends. She occasionally threw a finished shirt or pair of pants back at me, implying that they didn't meet her standards. Apparently, the goal was for my seven-year-old brother—one of the two male "suns" around which the women in our household were expected to orbit—to be the most wrinkle-free kid in his first-grade class.

This went on for months, but one day, I'd had it. My friends were outside, having fun, while I was inside, laboring under the pretense of training to be a "good wife." I already knew this odious task would NOT be a part of my future. No way. I began muttering, and then talking aloud, and finally, to get my mother's attention away from her phone gossiping, I began to yell.

"I am done with this!" I exclaimed. "These are not MY husband's shirts!" I said. "I didn't give birth to this child; these are YOUR son's jeans. YOU can iron them!"

My mother appeared back around the corner into the kitchen, phone cord in hand, with her mouth hanging open in a small *O*.

And down the hallway came my father.

Now my father is a big man. One who often threatened to hit you with his belt, though, in reality, he rarely caught you. Sure, you'd get a swat on the back of the head if you did something disrespectful, such as uttering a particularly good swear word or, later, while learning to drive, made a wrong turn somewhere. But beatings were rare.

Apparently, my outburst that morning was a DEFCON 1 event, because my father was pulling his belt out of his pants, ready to hand out a serious punishment.

Except he forgot one important thing. As he entered the kitchen, he faced an unexpected, and armed, opponent: a thirteen-and-a-half-year-old girl, flush with hormones, holding a smoldering electrical appliance.

He raised the belt. I calmly raised the iron.

He stopped dead. Did a double take. Then looked at my mother and said, "You handle this."

There was a long pause as she looked at me.

I unplugged the iron and walked away. And that was the end of my good wife lessons.

My husband has often wondered why, on our very first date, one of the questions I asked him was if he ironed his own shirts.

He said, "Of course."

I said, "That's a wise answer."

Depths of the Damned

by BONNIE JEAN FELDKAMP

My father threw me out of the house when I was eighteen. He could no longer deal with a rebellious teen. Neither one of us could recognize my cries for help, and though I tried to for some time, I cannot blame Dad for my choices. It is not his fault that I bounced from friend to friend and job to job. Nor is it his fault that when I ran out of friends, I bounced from bed to bed to keep warm. At the time, I didn't think there were any other options for me.

I appealed to my father several times over the course of a year to let me come back home. He was getting his life back after his divorce from my stepmother, and I was floundering on the streets. To quote my father, I "always have to learn the hard way."

That hard way came when I found a warm bed named Randy. I can pinpoint the dread in my heart when he reached his careless climax. I whispered, fearfully, "Did you just come inside me?"

A few weeks later I approached him with the news that I was pregnant. His message was clear: This was my problem.

The clinic waiting room resembled a beauty parlor. Women as old as forty and girls as young as fourteen. They were wives, mothers, and daughters. Not the desperate whores I expected.

I was on autopilot, responding only to direct orders. Pay the lady at the desk, next an ultrasound, and then deeper into the labyrinth, where my next destination was decorated in steel. The depths of hell, dressed up to play doctor. I undressed from the waist down then climbed into the metal chair. A nurse in scrubs entered. I pleaded with her: "Will you hold my hand?"

"Yes," she said gently as she placed a little rubber mask on me that barely covered my nose.

"Breathe in through your nose and out through your mouth," she said. The gas hissed in my nostrils.

The doctor stepped on the pedal that pivoted the chair, separated my legs, and dropped the seat away from my bottom. The nurse offered her hand as promised, and I gratefully accepted her odd latex-covered comfort. I felt the prick of a shot in my cervix, followed by the loud hum of heavy machinery. Strangely, it reminded me of a carnival generator kicking on at the start of a ride. Then I was yanked from my vision like a harvested crop. "Oh, God, it hurts"; I writhed with pain. My jaw dropped and I gasped for air, forgetting the gas in my nose. It seemed useless. We were doing this. I shut my eyes to block out the scenery and my knees collapsed to either side, reopening the passageway in surrender.

When the doctor finished, he stepped on the pedal to pivot me upright and left as silently as he had approached. I forced myself vertical and stood half naked while my brush with maternity dripped into a puddle on the floor.

After my allotted thirty minutes to recover, someone hustled me into a cab and sent me on my way. But where, exactly, was "my way"?

Once again, I had nowhere to go. I decided to make one last appeal to my father.

I dialed the pay phone tucked in the corner of the grocery by the front windows.

"This is John," my father answered.

"Dad?" I asked, desperate to steady my voice. I swallowed the lump in my throat and tried again. "Dad, it's me."

"Yeah?" he responded, indifferent.

I continued as fast as I could, "I'm sorry to bother you, but I don't have anywhere else to go." I exhaled a tear, sucked it back up and kept going. "I just had surgery, and I'm not supposed to be on my feet." I couldn't say the word.

"What kind of surgery?" he pressed, emotionless.

"Uh, female surgery," I stumbled, not wanting to give up my secret. I bit my lip and waited, hoping he wouldn't ask any more questions.

"Were you pregnant?" His heartbroken voice told me that he knew.

I couldn't hold on. "Ye-es," I answered with a release of emotion I could no longer restrain. His voice remained steady, and he kept it short. "Where are you?"

I gave him directions, hung up the phone, and ventured back out into the cold, unable to regain my composure. Hunched over and grasping my vacant belly, I sobbed. I was going home.

Hostage for a Prayer

by JULIE DANIS

"Julie, I want to say a novena for your upcoming job interview, but I need to ask you something first."

Mom rarely initiated a phone call from my hometown to Chicago, where I lived. So when her voice came over the receiver on a summer Saturday afternoon, I came to attention. It was 1979; I was a twenty-five-year-old recent grad school graduate looking for a job in a recession. Bring on divine intervention.

Mom regularly said novenas, Catholic prayers of petition or thanksgiving. She would retreat to her chair in the living room and read from her tattered prayer book, held together with rubber bands, while moving rosary beads through her fingers. Now she needed information before setting her intentions.

"Are you and Drew sleeping together?"

On the morning of my sister's wedding, three months before the novena call, Mom, wearing a pink robe and hair bonnet, walked into my bedroom and asked, "Have your feelings about premarital sex changed since you've started dating Drew?"

Drew was different from other boyfriends my parents had met. He called them by their first names, not Mr. and Mrs. Danis. He hugged them upon his first and all subsequent visits. He was from New York City—not the Midwest, like me—and had a swagger that broadcast a "take me as I am, I'm pretty cool" attitude.

This was the first time Mom and I had exchanged words about sex, unless you count the time she asked me if I had any questions about the Disney film *You Are a Woman Now.*

162

When my sister and her fiancé moved in together, before they were even engaged, my mom was upset, hurt, and disappointed. This living arrangement was a poor reflection on her as a mother, and she didn't want to fail again with me.

She was in luck. My feelings were unchanged. I had enjoyed sex before Drew and with Drew—maybe even more with Drew, but that doesn't count as changing. I could honestly say, "No, Mom they haven't."

Now, after Mom's first attempt to interrogate my sexual habits before the wedding, she was back to cross-examine. Perhaps she realized she hadn't asked the right question before. She didn't care about my feelings about sex; she just cared if I was having it.

I was being held hostage for a prayer. I had a choice: Tell the truth and don't get the prayer, or say anything other than yes and get the prayer. I wondered if the truth benefited either of us.

"What makes you ask, Mom?"

"When you were home for your sister's wedding, I heard Drew say that he sometimes rocked you to sleep."

"Oh, you must have misheard. He did buy me a cane rocker, though." Drew may have rocked me to sleep once or twice. But he would never have said something like that in front of my mother, even if they hugged and were on a first-name basis.

Mom and I stumbled through the conversation as I maneuvered it away from sex to the job interview and then to a close. Somehow, I evaded or obscured the truth. I'm not sure if she prayed a novena—I didn't get the job—but the topic of my virginity remained unexamined for eleven years, until David.

I met David in 1991 on one of my frequent trips back home to check on my parents. Dad's forgetfulness had devolved into dementia, and Mom's anxiety, blood pressure, and needs had increased accordingly.

Mom liked David. He called her Mrs. Danis, was not at all hug-y, and ambled instead of swaggered. As far she knew, when I came home, I slept at my brother and sister-in-law's house, in my niece's bedroom. Until one Sunday morning when she called, looking for me.

"She's not here, Mom," my sister-in-law said.

"Where is she?"

"She stayed at David's."

"Why?"

"Because she's thirty-six and a grown woman?"

When I called Mom later that day, she asked, "Why did you change?"

"I'm an adult," I said, not knowing what else to say. I hadn't changed; I'd been found out.

Mom sighed over the phone. I don't know what weighed on her more. Lies. Sex. Or something completely unrelated, such as her arrhythmia or Dad's decline. It doesn't matter. Our relationship didn't suffer and—best of all—once the truth was out, we never spoke of the topic again. Thank heaven.

Virtue Signaling

by KATHLEEN JONES

Passing judgment on the domestic and moral failings of other women was one of my mother's favorite hobbies. She enjoyed it, I imagine, the way some women gained satisfaction from macramé or needlepoint. The end results of her labors were neither useful nor pretty, but that didn't stop her from displaying them in the house.

She *tsk-tsked* her way through my formative years, whispering behind her hand at those who broke her rules for ladylike deportment. No one was spared her critical gaze, but at least those who lived outside of the house didn't have to hear about it. I wasn't so lucky and learned early that to ignore my mother's edicts—or, worse, question them—was to invite her chilly disapproval.

Her rules, though infinite in their variations and fetishistic in their detail, could be rendered down to one irrefutable law: Good morals equal good housekeeping. Cleanliness may be next to godliness, but virginity is its conjoined twin. If my brothers had codes to follow, they were masculine, mysterious, and did not include vacuuming. My older sister and I lived under a tyranny of neatness and were tasked with living up to our mother's domestic and social expectations. A Good Girl kept her bed made and her mouth shut; never used tampons, had sex, or visited a gynecologist until marriage; never left the house without wearing a slip under her skirt; and never, *ever* drank beer. A Good Mother made piecrust and pasta sauce from scratch, never placed the milk carton directly on the dinner table (it must be poured into a separate pitcher first), and never, *ever* put her children down for naps with dirty feet.

My sister shouldered the burden of expectation more easily, being the oldest, tidy by nature, and eager to please. I, however, was not a willing apprentice to the domestic arts, and I bucked and buckled under their yoke. I was messy, mouthy, and the source of my mother's chronic exasperation. As a teenager I was deemed "lazy," "unladylike," and, after losing my virginity at seventeen, "damaged goods."

By the time my mother declared that no man would ever marry me because I wasn't a virgin, I had done the math (*everyone* had done the math) and spoke aloud that glaring, hidden truth: My mother was pregnant when my father married her. Up the stick. *Pregnant.*

I wanted a moment of reckoning. I had found the loose thread on my mother's hem, and I wanted to pull, *hard*, until she stood before me in naked honesty. I received instead the cold fury of her silence. What I needed was her unqualified love and some practical advice.

But no. When I left for college a year later, my mother sent me off with a harvest gold Hamilton Beach clothes iron and little else—no typewriter, no roll of quarters for the laundry, no wisdom for coping with a difficult roommate. An iron.

This academic dowry made no sense: was it the ticket to college success? It certainly wouldn't help me land a husband, since that ship had sailed. Perhaps I could use it to smooth out my rough edges, to flatten myself into starched respectability. If I hadn't turned out immaculate, couldn't I at least look immaculately turned out?

My mother began unraveling her own life when she was forty-seven. After a twenty-nine-year marriage, she divorced my father and began living with (and then married) a man who made her only slightly less unhappy. Two days after her divorce was finalized, my mother was diagnosed with cancer. She was dead at fifty-four.

I know that my mother's choices were completely unrelated to her cancer diagnosis, but I wonder if she knew that. Since she judged others with such zeal—I understand now, out of the desperate fear of being judged herself—she must have also turned that critical eye inward. How does one live with the weight of so much shame?

I hated my mother for her hypocrisy and for the shame she passed down to me. I am the lucky one, though, and struggled out from beneath its weight to a place of self-acceptance. I wish I could tell her I forgive her. I would invite her to my cluttered, comfortable home to meet my husband and children. I might offer her my own domestic advice: Hang your clothes right from the dryer, and the wrinkles fall out on their own.

Salem Witches

by BRENDA MURPHY

You can't read much about the Salem witchcraft trials without coming across the sexualized image of the fallen woman. Unless she was ancient or, in the case of one of them, four years old, a seventeenth-century female person who was accused of covenanting with the Devil was generally thought of in terms of illicit sexuality. She was to be feared by pious men, not only for the power she was granted by the Devil to harm them, their families, their animals, and their crops and goods but also for the mysterious sexual power she might exert over them.

Odd allusions to this power pepper the official court documents. Stephen Bittford testified that the specters of Rebecca Nurse and Elizabeth Procter had come to his bedchamber at midnight and held his head, which gave him a great pain in the neck for three days. William Allen testified that the specter of Sarah Good had come to his bedchamber one night with a strange light and sat on his foot, but both light and specter vanished when he managed to kick her off. Elizabeth Hubbard, who worked at the village doctor's house, said in front of the neighbors one evening that she saw Sarah Good's specter standing on the table, barefooted, bare legged, and bare breasted. When Elizabeth cried out that she would kill the nasty slut if she had something to strike her with, Samuel Sibley obliged by beating the air with his staff until Elizabeth said he had struck Sarah's specter across the back and almost killed her. Testifying against Susannah Martin, Robert Downer said that as he lay alone in his bed one night, a cat came in through the window, jumped on the bed, took fast hold of his throat, and "lay hard upon" him for a considerable time until he managed to send it packing by calling out "avoid thou she-devil" in the name of the Father, Son, and Holy Ghost.

This kind of thing is what we expect to find in the records of the Salem witchcraft episode. After all, witchcraft was defined as congress with the Devil, which implies illicit sexuality. But as public opinion about the witchcraft trials shifted from sympathy for the accusers to sympathy for the accused, a similar shift occurred in the perception of the sexual threat. As more and more of Rebecca Nurse's neighbors signed petitions and testified in support of her good character, the image of the saintly and grandmotherly figure that is familiar to us from Arthur Miller's *The Crucible* emerged. Likewise, Elizabeth Procter, a salty, sharp-tongued tavern keeper, became the upright matriarch of the Procter clan. On the other hand, the "afflicted children," the girls and young women who had accused these women, became increasingly suspect.

When the governor outlawed the use of testimony involving specters in the witchcraft trials, the whole house of cards collapsed, and the young women who had been treated with universal respect and deference because of their ability to see the "invisible world" fell from grace with a thud. Suddenly, they were no longer child possessors of a gift from God, but deranged women under a delusion of Satan. Along with this fall came the shadow of illicit sexuality. Most of the young women left the area after the trials, but rumors about their sexual transgressions were still rife. Whether it was being punished for fornication in Maine, having birthed a child out of wedlock in New Hampshire, being excommunicated for adultery in Boston, or being driven from Providence for prostitution, these women's stories had a sexual taint that persisted in historical accounts. In her well-known 1949 popular history of the witchcraft trials, *The Devil in Massachusetts*, Marion L. Starkey simply wrote that some of the girls, not explicitly named in the history books, "went unmistakably bad."

There were plenty of male accusers and accused in the Salem witch-craft trials. Men were accused of brutal beatings and even of multiple murders. Giles Cory, who is known for being pressed to death for standing mute and refusing to plead in court, was accused of pressing a man to death with his boots as well as beating a servant, a "natural fool," to death. John Willard was accused of beating his wife and murdering thirteen people, including seven children. But the men were not accused of rape or other sexual molestation. Stories of sexual transgression don't cling to them. That narrative is reserved for fallen women.

A Single Woman

by BARBARA COOLEY

By the age of eighteen, I had disappointed my mother more than my three brothers, father, and *The Joy of Cooking* combined. She had invested in me all her antiquated visions of womanhood, and each milestone had its own rite of passage. Sweet Sixteen was celebrated with good luggage. High school graduation was supposed to be lipstick, pearls, and high heels. In college I would learn business and secretarial skills. My hope chest would be secured with a lock, awaiting the man who would take on her difficult daughter. My wedding night would mark the end of my closely guarded chastity, and it would be the magic key to that hope chest full of delicate kitchen linens and dusty ideas of womanhood. "Yes! Yes! YES! Irish linen tea towels!"

When I marked high school graduation with a tie-dyed T-shirt, bell-bottom jeans, and a discarded bra, Mother's tight lips spelled disappointment. My decision to delay college while attempting to find myself (as a barmaid in a college tavern) caused her heart to palpitate. The birth control pills she stumbled across in my purse rendered her speechless. Conversations with other mothers about their daughters' traditional paths—marriages and motherhood—broke like cold waves over her simple dreams. And so, in my mid-twenties, when I chose to use a small inheritance as the down payment on a house, the last of my mother's proscriptive designs for my life shattered into pieces at the base of an empty pedestal. The key to the front door of my first house belonged in the hands of some nameless, faceless Mr. Right, but there I was, about to stride across the threshold of my first house without even a Mr. Wrong.

In spite of the Equal Credit Opportunity Act of 1974, mandating women's legal right to credit even when single, lending committees at most banks were still composed nearly exclusively of men. I anticipated that but was still unprepared for what would happen at the closing. The legal papers were stacked on the boardroom table, and pens and water glasses were in front of every seat. The bankers, as starched as their shirts, were seated there along with my Realtor, me, and the document preparer, the only other woman in the room. At twenty-five, I was an adjunct faculty at the local community college while continuing my own education and working part-time as a server to make ends meet. Logically, I knew the monthly mortgage payment would actually be less than my current rent; as a fierce feminist, I relished the thought of owning my own house.

I was taken aback, however, by the first document awaiting my signature. It contained a legal description of the property, the terms of the mortgage, and a description of me, the buyer: "Barbara Cooley, a single woman." Stunned, I glanced around the room and mumbled something about Hester Prynne, but the men didn't seem to get it. So I followed up with a quip about how the label seemed more like a branding than a description.

"Will I be legally required to remain single as long as I own the house?" I wondered aloud. "How will I look with a scarlet 'SW' emblazoned on my chest?" I mused. No one laughed.

A couple of the men shifted in their chairs until my real estate agent explained Michigan's dower rights law, which protected any assets a single woman might bring into a marriage. This meant she could sell, rent, or bequeath such property without her husband being entitled to any of it or even knowing about it. That law required that I be so designated in order to protect my rights to the property should I later marry.

"It's an antiquated law," my Realtor said, but I was secretly gratified with the power and security it gave me. For once the law protected rather than restricted or subjugated women.

While I laughed with my friends over the legal description of me, my mother resigned herself to her only daughter being branded a single woman indefinitely, a homeowner with no bra, no virginity, and no husband.

"But Barbara, there's no longer any reason for you to marry," my mother moaned.

"Oh, Mother, there's still one." I responded.

"Children?" she asked, hopeful.

"Love," I replied.

I let her cling tightly to that one last vestige of traditional femininity, but when I did meet and fall in love with a wonderful man, I felt duty-bound to inform her: I had proposed to him.

Scar

by Jane Cook

I have a scar on my left elbow. Sometimes I forget that it's there, but sometimes it itches or aches, reminding me of a long-ago fall.

I've loved horses for as long as I can remember. As a child, I lived on a dairy farm. Though I loved all the animals, my heart ached for a horse. Unfortunately, unless they could pull their weight, horses were a luxury we could not afford. Dad had his tractor, so all I could do was dream.

After my folks had to sell the farm, I continued to dream, even though we no longer had barns and pastureland. As a teenager, I worked on tobacco farms, using my wages to pay room and board, to save for college, and to take horseback riding lessons.

My lessons were with Mrs. Wells, a tiny, wizened lady with a booming voice. She had been around horses her entire life. She could certainly handle horses, but she didn't have patience for teenagers.

She put me on Fog, a big gray half-draft horse who was gentle and patient. I fell in love. As I trotted around the ring on Fog's broad back, Mrs. Wells would scream, "SIT UP STRAIGHT! KEEP YOUR HEELS DOWN!" I tried hard, but the harder I tried, the more I failed, and the sterner and louder Mrs. Wells got. I may not have been her best student, but I never fell off Fog's broad back.

After college, while working at the University of Connecticut, I saw that the Animal Sciences department offered summer horseback riding lessons. I signed up immediately.

My teacher, Janice, was calm and patient, but I could still hear Mrs. Wells's admonitions, so I sat up straight and kept my heels down. One day, a friend came to watch my class. As we trotted around the outdoor ring, Janice told my friend, "Jane may not have the best form, but she's the best rider of all my students. She looks like she was born on a horse." When I heard that, my confidence soared.

The class consisted of several teenage girls and one young man. The teenagers were learning to ride so they could compete in horse shows. I already knew how to ride. I was taking the class so I could spend time with horses.

Halfway through the summer, Janice told us it was time to start jumping. The teenagers were thrilled. I wasn't particularly interested in learning to jump, but I figured that when I finally got my own horse, we might need to jump over a fallen log out on a trail.

We started class as usual—walking, then trotting, and finally cantering around the ring. After we warmed up, Janice put out a low fence to prepare for jumping.

Though Janice had said I was the best rider, I was nervous. I waited in line and watched carefully as the teenagers took their turns, clearing that low jump with ease. Too soon, it was my turn. I gathered up my courage and started cantering toward the jump. I heard Janice call out, "Get on the right lead," just as my horse started over the jump. The next thing I knew, I was out of the saddle, falling to the ground, landing hard on my left elbow.

The young man jumped off his mare and ran to me. As he knelt down over me, my elbow was throbbing and bleeding, but my ankle hurt much worse. In his haste to help, he had put his full weight on it.

"I was a medic in the army. Are you OK? Can you hear me? How many fingers am I holding up?"

I answered, "You're kneeling on my ankle. That really hurts."

"Oh, I'm sorry." He blushed and jumped up. "Are you OK?"

"I'm fine," I answered as I scrambled to my feet.

My ankle felt better, but my elbow was bloody and sore. I headed home to nurse my elbow and my wounded pride. How could I have fallen off? Wasn't I the best rider in the class? But I went back every week till the end of the summer and kept trying.

Now, every so often when I rub my left elbow, I can feel the half dollar–sized scar. It reminds me that no matter how good you are, you can always fall. But you'll be all right, just as long as you keep getting up.

Good as Nude

by ERIN BROCHU

There was no line in the sand differentiating the nude beach from the textile beach, or maybe there was, but we were too busy wondering how comfortable it could actually be for the two guys playing Frisbee with their dicks out.

It was chilly, but winter in San Diego was like the equivalent of spring in New England, so it was 65 degrees and sunny. We tried to mask our innocence and feign belonging, but curiosity got the better of us as we looked around. A few people opted to keep their garments on, while others basked unabashedly in the glory of their birthday suits. There were men who lay out on towels—I hope they remembered to put sunscreen on *everything*—and women that lounged around with pubic hair that was untrimmed and untamed. Old men with micro-penises strutted along the sand with the confidence of the lifeguards on *Baywatch*.

The beach stretched about a mile and was tucked away beneath massive stone bluffs. "In The Buff Under The Bluffs!" is their official slogan, or it would be if it were up to me. Although everyone else seemed comfortable, we decided that it didn't make sense for us to go au naturel, considering we didn't bring anything to lie out on. Walking on the nude beach holding all of our clothes in a bundle felt like we were trying too hard to be naked.

After our two-mile stroll took us back to the line that separated the robed from the disrobed, we turned around to have one last look at the naturalists. Now that we were back in the land of the clothed, we somehow felt like our right to be nude had been stripped from us. We were jealous of their ability to be uninhibited and disappointed in

177

ourselves for our lack of courage in showing a little booty. We convinced ourselves that we would come back, but that's like saying "Let's do this again sometime!" after an awful date—it's never going to happen again.

"Are we really not going to do this?" Maddie asked. "I personally couldn't forgive myself if I left here without taking *something* off." If she were any character from *Sex and the City*, it would be Samantha, which sums up her character development in life pretty well. A "try-sexual" known for her love of men and their love of her, she's never had trouble getting a date but is never emotionally involved; she's too busy for that.

"Now that we've made it all the way back, I feel bummed not being able to say we did it." Brooke has been beautiful her whole life, often remembered for her skinny frame and pretty features, as well as her affinity for snacking without gaining any weight. She had just recently found out she was expecting, so she had the pregnancy boobs without the responsibility of a bump; she was winning the lottery. With motherhood on the horizon, I guess she was searching for one last youthful story to be able to tell her daughter one day.

"Yeah, but it also feels like a little more trouble than it's worth to take everything off just to put it back on." In my defense, I was wearing the bathing suit equivalent to Houdini's straitjacket. I had this skintight one-piece, long-sleeved bathing suit on under my jacket that I couldn't even put on without someone helping with the zipper. Brooke and Maddie were just in their bikinis with jackets flung on top.

"I think if we don't do it, we're seriously gonna regret it," Brooke said as she untied her bikini top. I looked at Maddie, who was already holding hers in her hand. A few years ago I was self-diagnosed with Fear of Missing Out, an incurable affliction, so I knew I was as good as nude.

"Okay, somebody's gotta help me out of this thing." I took my arm out of my jacket as Maddie got to work on my zipper. Brooke started peeling the damp spandex material off my skin until I was freed from its embrace.

"Oh my God, this is amazing!" Maddie shrieked. "Whoever invented clothes needs to come and talk to me; they have some serious explaining to do."

"Maybe if I can keep this boob hidden, no one will be able to see how uneven they are," I said as I looked down at my girls. Even though they're twins, Lefty has always been ahead of her sister; she developed early.

"Erin, look up," Brooke said. "No one's even looking at us." She was right. No one was even looking at themselves. I had always thought of nudity as an incredibly vulnerable act, but here it seemed as unremarkable as going to the grocery store.

"Come on, Erin! This is our confidence moment!" Maddie added, tugging at my sleeve. I reluctantly let the front of my fluffy safety net fly open. The ocean breeze rushed over parts of my body that had never seen sunshine.

With each step we gained the courage to take more off until we were completely unveiled. Soon enough, we were no longer three friends walking on the beach. We were the Pink Ladies on their first day of school at Rydell High. We were stars of the red carpet at the Met Gala, our cellulite was couture and our love handles designer. We weren't sure when we were going to run out of nude beach, so we stayed in line with the wrinkled man hobbling on the opposite side of the sand wearing only a baseball cap. When he stopped to turn around, it was time to exit the runway. We stood with our feet in the water for a few minutes before stepping back into our fabric prisons. Putting our clothes back on felt perverse and wrong. They felt like some cruel deception, one that forced women to feel guilty for not being the same jean size in every store or made all the hours we spend picking out what to wear feel like a complete waste of time.

There's never been a dress that made me feel more beautiful than I did that day. Being on that nude beach was the first time I felt every insecurity about my body disappear, it was swept away in that salty breeze. I'd never seen more of my friends than I did that day, but I've never noticed them less. We only worried about how much fun we were having, playing in the sand like toddlers allowed to take their overalls off. It gave us a renewed sense of self-possession to bear no possessions, and we'll be able to tell Brooke's baby that friends will always be willing to take the shirts off their own back for each other.

Getting Up

I WILL NOT DIE HERE.

The words scream through my head. Pain pierces my skull and hip, the frigid ice biting the exposed skin on my neck and hands. I lie on the ground staring up into the black night sky as freezing rain pelts my face.

GET UP.

Except I can't. The pain is excruciating. By the porch light I see Emma, our golden retriever puppy, who needed a nighttime potty break. Her legs are going in every direction as she tries to get traction on the icy path beside me. I stretch and push her onto the deep snowbank. She pops up, looks at me. It's clearly my turn. I gradually roll over, crawl onto the snow, each move sending a searing daggerlike pain through my body. I wrap Emma's leash around my hand and slowly stand. We walk a few short steps, leaving me breathless. Emma's relieved to finally pee. I'm afraid of what exactly I have broken. The world around me sways.

MY FACE IS FREEZING.

I feel the puppy tugging on the fur of my winter boot, waking me. Good girl, Emma. I realize I've fallen face down in the snow. The ice-covered snow beneath me seeps through my open coat and pink-striped pajamas. I know in my bones that I will die here if I don't move.

GET UP.

I push myself up again and begin the shuffle to the front door, avoiding the slick, treacherous walkway. Opening the door is a relief. I made it. I didn't die outside. I don't try to take my boots off as I stare up the dark stairwell. I can't do this. I call out for my husband. Was that more than a whisper? Instinctively, I know he can't hear me over his white noise machine, but I am praying he can. I slowly start to crawl up on my hands and knees. Halfway up, I carefully lay my head down on the carpeted tread as the stairs begin to tilt.

GET UP.

I open my eyes to see Emma sitting next to me, waiting. How long have I been here? We creep up the rest of the way. Using the banister, I pull myself up. I stagger down the long hall to my bedroom. No words come to me as I wake my husband by shaking his foot. Startled, he begins asking a million questions. All I can mumble is "I'm hurt" as I hobble over to return the puppy safely to her crate. I can do this. I will finish what I started.

GET UP.

My husband is standing above me, a look of confusion on his face. My head and torso somehow landed in the crate with Emma. I inch myself out and lie on the floor, feeling little puppy kisses on my hand through the bars. He's still asking questions, pleading with me to stand up, but I can't. I try to answer, but nothing makes sense. Try to explain that if I rise, I will fall. Again.

Now, all the lights are on, and my three boys wake up with the mayhem. Their worried faces stare down at me as I try to reassure them. My husband calls 9-1-1 and I ask my oldest to take his younger twin brothers into their bedroom and put on cartoons. Fear of going to the hospital mid-pandemic grips me and I frantically tell my husband, "I need two masks!" When the paramedics arrive, one of them gently tells me that he is going to support me, promising to hold me up if I lose consciousness. And he does.

Meanwhile, it takes an emergency crew to plow our street while the courageous paramedics slip and slide as they salt the walkway to get me safely to the ambulance. With all the commotion, I miss the three sweet, concerned faces in the upstairs window watching their mom being taken away.

KEEP RISING.

It's been a year of pain, frustration, therapy, and questioning when I will fully recover. The doctors told me I was lucky; I could have been paralyzed. No one mentioned how much longer I could have survived unconscious in the snow. They said I have to be patient, that the wounds will eventually heal. With each passing day, however, it becomes more like a distant memory, seeming like a dream or an old nightmare, gifting me with the knowledge that I am strong enough to always get back up.

Rituals & Resurgence

by CARA E. KILGALLEN

I collapsed on the cold vinyl floor of a barren hospital bathroom after frantically flushing the toilet for hours while several psychiatric health-care professionals struggled to restrain me. Just one further flush, I believed due to my obsessive-compulsive mindset, would prevent the loss of countless loved ones. On the flip side, if I didn't continue my frenetic flushing, the entire world would suffer under my watch.

Obsessive-compulsive disorder (OCD) had offered me a false sense of power at the same time that it stripped me of all control; I couldn't stop flushing.

The handsome male nurse, who happened to be my first crush—I was a ten-year-old patient at the time—tried to lighten things up.

"Mayor Dinkins [in 1989, Dinkins was mayor of New York City] will shut off our electricity if we continue to waste water," said Rob the heartthrob.

"Dinkins won't have to turn off the power," grunted the physician's assistant; "She's already flicked the lights on and off thousands of times."

Hours earlier, I had abandoned my light-switching ritual and transitioned to toilets. The toilet flushing not only made me feel fallen and utterly lacking in control but also literally led to my fall as I collapsed on the hospital floor in a desperate struggle against the nurses' firm grasp.

The room was damp, dark, and dusty, though its superficially sanitized floors gave the appearance of cleanliness. To this day, I can still smell the combination of Clorox and Lysol that the cleaners—who visited the psych ward once a day—used to sanitize the place. One of the patients had peed earlier in the community room, and I remember feeling simultaneously sorry for the staff who had to wipe up the urine and relieved that it did not cover the floor over which I had sprawled my body.

OCD creates a perpetual cycle of rituals in many patients, and I certainly was no exception. Throughout my three-month stay at St. Vincent's (the West Village hospital that sadly no longer exists, despite rescuing the city during 9/11 and the AIDS crisis), I performed a wide array of ritualistic behaviors: flashing lights on and off; touching electrical sockets; swallowing thousands of times before bed; and, of course, toilet flushing. Heavy medication and intense psychotherapy reduced my rituals over time and helped me gain control of my impulses, but I remained tormented by the urge to continue them even after my discharge in December 1989.

Prior to my hospital admittance three months earlier, I had become a pariah at my Manhattan private school. My OCD was met with such kindness and compassion from many, but others freaked out, and some spread rumors of illegal drug use. There is no doubt that my need to spin in circles during recess, or the occasional conversation with myself as a fifth grader, made my peers and their families frightened to interact with me.

I felt totally and utterly fallen, both in school and even inside St. Vincent's walls. Although some fellow patients on Floor 6 of the psychiatric department on West Twelfth Street had far more severe conditions than mine, I was the lone wolf with OCD, and my compulsive complications made me feel far more powerless than others—even young boys screaming their heads off—at times.

The irrational nature of my disorder triggered in me perpetual impulses to perform ridiculous rituals, which had the potential to cause danger to myself. One moment that stands out involved a fellow in-patient, the ten-year-old daughter of crack-addicted parents who tried desperately to convince me that my rituals were lacking in rationality.

"You do not have to touch the electrical sockets," the young girl who became my friend reassured me. "I know you think that something bad will happen, but really you might hurt yourself if you continue doing this." Even at the time, I found this statement remarkable from a girl—let's call her Katie—who had been so damaged and neglected throughout her life.

Katie helped bring me away from the electrical sockets and into the light. Finally, on perhaps my fiftieth flush, something suddenly stopped me from continuing. Rob the heartthrob may have had something to do with my discontinuation of this ritual, but I distinctly recall a release—something catapulted me off the floor and away from the toilet's roaring waters. I no longer felt as though my OCD was drowning me, and I began to breathe again.

Swept Off My Feet by Luis

by CAROL GIEG

My husband, Luis, relishes his morning routine, especially the time spent making and drinking his coffee. While he's downstairs, I go to my computer and click on a link, which opens to a yoga class I haven't tried before. My current practice includes meditation and is forty years old. Only recently have I noticed its flagging efficacy.

I want to set new goals and rise to new occasions.

Both meditation and yoga have become the lingo of my friends lately. They extol the virtues (and neuroscience confirmation) that merely twelve minutes a day of meditation have been proven to delay cognitive decline, or possibly slow the progression in those already compromised. One friend pointed out that even the insurance company Kaiser Permanente is offering health education classes in meditation.

What have I got to lose? I thought.

I turned to my cousin, Durga.

Durga has lived for forty-plus years in a community of people who are followers of Swami Paramahansa Yogananda (of *Autobiography of a Yogi* fame). Theirs is one of the few successful holdouts from the many such groups formed during the 1960s. Members live by Yogananda's teachings not just in words but also in actions and in unequivocal support for one another.

Yoga and meditation are integral practices in their way of life.

It is possible that I need to find pathways to stillness, to living in the moment, to releasing my body and mind from anxiety and stress.

My cousin responded to my request for help by sending me links to exercises that she felt would be just what I needed.

I believed they would be too—until I attempted to follow along with the finely tuned and muscular instructor through different poses. Disappointed with myself, I simply could not get my body to adequately emulate his movements. I felt failure replace hope; I felt crestfallen rather than elated.

My Standing Crane is on its last legs; my Downward Dog stretches out for a nap; my Plank erodes into a hammock.

I'm about as flexible as a wine barrel stave. I don't like to fail, especially in public, and am grateful that I'm dealing with an online class.

When I learn that yoga is meant to be a "preparation" for meditation, I decide I've proven to be too evolved for yoga. I fast-forward into the more exalted meditation. It doesn't occur to me at the time that "fast-forwarding" is not exactly the point of yoga and meditation.

Perhaps it's not surprising, then, that I bump up against the difficulty I have in "releasing my mind" from all thought.

I discover that meditation requires greater effort than working myself into the physique required for maintaining different yoga poses. At least with yoga, I don't have to "quiet" anything.

Finally, it's time to surrender my Buddhist aspirations. I decide to reward myself by spending more time with my Luis.

Having come to this conclusion, I rejoin him in the kitchen, where he is swaying back and forth to Tia McGraff, a smile on his face. He is oblivious to everything else.

Wanting to share in his state, I reach out my hands to him. He draws them to his chest and we lean into each other. I sing along and shadow his movements. Each crescendo of the music is accompanied by his arms raising my hands in a fanlike motion.

It's all I can do to keep on dancing as visions of the future lurk. I am losing him to dementia.

It occurs to me, as I am in his arms, that my suffering is selfish. I look at his smiling face and feel his hands holding me tightly, spinning me around with him across the floor with effortless movements.

When the last notes sound, he spreads his arms wide, and our arms move together as if we are birds about to take flight. He plants a kiss on my lips. I am willing to forgo practices others use to help ground them. Together with my Luis.

A Calculated Fall

by MISTY L. KNIGHT

The snow had fallen, almost five feet in some areas, covering the world like a glorious blanket—the grime and gray from previous snows obliterated with a fresh coat of white. I saw it as a chance to be free. Expend positive energy, drink cocoa, and build a snowman. Despite the burden of having to face clearing the driveway and sidewalks alone, I felt nothing but relief. He was gone. Banished to the other side of the country on a research trip that I insisted he take because I couldn't take any more of him. The only weight was that of the snow I shoveled and, comparatively, it was light.

A few weeks before, he fell. Drunk again, he had fallen down the stairs and left a gaping hole in the drywall at the landing. After making sure he was still alive, I gingerly slipped around him and packed bags for me and the boys so they wouldn't have to witness this fall. His drunken antics had almost ruined the holiday season for our two boys and most certainly had for me. It should have warned me what was to come that year, but I thought the trip and some time away would bring just the healing we needed. Instead, he saw my social media posts about the snow and immediately texted to accuse me of making him out to be "a bad guy" because he was in sunny California while we toiled. My joy for the fallen snow now leveled as an accusation.

Additional accusations continued throughout the year, not that this was different from the past twenty-plus. I was talking badly about him. I was destroying his reputation. I was ruining his relationship with the kids. I was causing his behavior. Except, I wasn't. I neither said nor did any of those things, but I fell for it. I fell for the guilt trap. It was my fault. If only I was a better wife, a better mother, and not such a fallen woman. I fell for the gaslighting. My friends thought I was scum. I wasn't good at my job. He wasn't using his body to trap me in rooms while he raged at me, he just didn't want me to keep avoiding the problem we were discussing. It was my fault that he had to hide gin in the ceiling insulation.

December of that year had a chilling end. The first blow was a shock, and his haunting laughter as he stalked me while I ran rang in my ears. I fell and fell into a deeper and deeper depression as I realized that the marriage I had worked so hard to preserve had to end. I fell with each blow, physical and emotional. So, at that nadir, I crawled away.

For years after, I became the fallen woman I was raised to deride and scorn. I fell when I drank. I fell to the floor in tears, guilt, and despair. I sought comfort in a series of trysts that provided no safe padding. The fall to my rock bottom had the same impact as the punches that landed that final night so many years before. I fell to the point at which I could take no more and decided to stop the falling with a definitive end. And I survived.

The next several years were a slow and steady climb out of the depths until, at last, I was a healthy and whole woman. Present for my family. Present for my friends. Present for my work. Most importantly, present for myself. Until I fell again.

I didn't want to fall anymore; I never imagined that I would. I fell deeply, but in a slow and measured way. Much like a stunt double or action actor who learns to take a calculated fall. I fell for someone who is kind. Loving. Genuine. Gentle. Amazing.

This time? The fall is perfectly wonderful.

Psycho Killer, Twelve Years Old

by CECILIA GIGLIOTTI

I come from angry people. They carry their rage in their shoulders, their wrists, the napes of their necks, the corners of their mouths. For the most part, it doesn't manifest beyond a CD rack full of hard-edged track listings. For the most part, they try to handle it in the privacy of their own psyches. For the most part, they succeed.

They wouldn't describe themselves as angry. That's how you know they are. Still, even their control has its limits. My extrovert father expresses his anger through jokes and strong opinions on matters of little objective importance, appearing like a barb or a blow. My mother's anger is insidious, threaded through a narrative of uncertainty and displacement, appearing like poison. This is an anecdote of her anger, and how it came to me.

But first, if I may: Talking Heads.

Both my parents were fans of the band from early in their career. The thinking man's rock stars, as they came to be known. I heard them in flashes throughout my youth, then got a fuller picture when I watched *Stop Making Sense* in my mid-teens. I remember seeing a production of *Macbeth* with a friend at age seventeen, commenting on the soundtrack (chosen by the cast) that filtered into the theater between acts. It was then that I listened, really listened, to "Psycho Killer" for the first time, tuning out all else, disappearing, recognizing something, digging it up. A memory—not of *Stop Making Sense*.

I was twelve. Maybe eleven. Mom and I had braved the summer temperatures to run an errand at the local YWCA, where I had taken

Saturday dance classes for eight years before switching to musical theater. I had been socially maladjusted offstage the whole time. En route back to the parking lot, we encountered a former classmate and her mother. I liked this girl but was apprehensive about an out-of-context exchange. Social interactions were typically disastrous in front of Mom; I got sidetracked by her eyes on me, her tangible investment in my belonging. She didn't mean to put undue pressure on me, but trying to succeed for two was exhausting. Here, now, I decided better to try *to* fail than to try *and* fail. I would end this thing before it began. Kill it before it became something I could screw up.

I guess you could call it an exchange the four of us had, my mumbling and lack of eye contact throwing any chance of sincere conversation. There was a relief of sorts as our acquaintances went their way, but I remember it hazed, blank, like the relief of death. When they were out of sight, Mom turned to me with something in her eyes I had never seen and said, "Cecilia, would it kill you, every once in a while, to be a bit *human*?"

Hearing the song through tinny theater speakers hit me with something like a PTSD flashback. I wouldn't be a full-fledged fan for several years yet, but I knew that, for a few minutes, in the empty YWCA parking lot on a scorching afternoon, I had spent time inside this psycho killer's head. *"Ce que j'ai fais . . . ce qu'elle a dit."* "What I did . . . what she said."

I'm sure in that moment, I opened my mouth with some impulse toward self-defense, but I don't remember coming up with anything. What could I say? I had no explanation for why I was the way I was. I had no excuses, only neuroses. And I didn't kill people, only hopes.

I don't know if my mother is angrier than my father; their unique histories of pain peak at different points in their lives. I do know that she forgives him where she cannot forgive herself. Part of this is that she feels the world forgives him where it does not forgive her, and that he deserves forgiveness where she does not. She casts herself as the villain of her family's story—convinced that she antagonized everyone she met in a New England town masquerading as a city, that she appeared belligerent and combative beside her easygoing husband and growing kids, that others had to try harder to see her good side, that her record of fighting for justice had painted her with a bad brush.

It turns out, an angry woman begot a livid child. If that day I saw her as a villain, she was the lesser villain of the two of us.

Falling in Love while Falling Apart

by HIEDI BUDWILL WOODS

Lying in bed, I watched my tummy move with my baby's kicks. I wanted to cover his face with kisses. Bringing two fingers to my lips, I kissed them instead, transferring them to the places where he was kicking. Yes, I love my husband, my cat, and my family. But this was different. I adored a human that I didn't even know.

Always prepared and organized, I planned a three-month leave from work after my son's birth. Envisioning blissful perfect days, I would breastfeed and take a restorative nap, walk in the sunshine, hang out with Daddy, read a book to the baby. The baby was healthy; I only gained weight in my tummy; I had energy and continued with exercise and working full-time.

The prenatal yoga video I did weekly was a favorite. The instructor's soothing voice purred, "Now place your hands on your belly and say I love you." My arms encircled the bump and a wave of love poured over me like a tsunami—a rush of peace, happiness, and completeness rolled into one.

We planned a natural birth, but after hours of trying, the doctor said it was time for a Caesarian. The baby was having some distress. Thankfully, everything was fine. We spent a week in the hospital, recovering from surgery, and then T and I went home. I was looking forward to those blissful days. The reality was very different, and that is when I fell apart.

To make things easier, my in-laws were staying with us and my husband was home. Taking care of a baby with help—doable but tiring;

just sleep when the baby does—hah! An average night's sleep was four hours off and on, no daytime naps. Aching jaw from clenched teeth; stomach constantly churning; a nervous feeling for no reason. Staring at the foldable stroller and having no idea how to collapse it and put it in the car. I had seen it done—why couldn't I do it? Once in the car, I had no desire to sing along to the radio. Another simple joy was gone. I felt inadequate. My organizational and multitasking skills had disappeared. As each day dawned, I would lie in bed, not knowing how I was going to get through it. I couldn't take a deep breath.

What was happening to me?

I had always been able to get it done. Either as a Dean's List student at UConn or moving across the country with no job or place to live. I was capable, smart, and healthy. Not afraid of new adventures, I had traveled extensively. I changed industries three times to find a successful career path. And yet at forty I stood in my kitchen unable to make dinner while my son slept peacefully nearby. Being overwhelmed by a package of ground turkey was not normal. This wasn't the "baby blues" you read about in books—a temporary condition of mood swings. This was debilitating and frightening.

Postpartum anxiety sucks.

Even though I was falling apart, T brought me joy and hope. After a nighttime bottle and change, I would re-swaddle him. The feeling of calm that swept across his face was beautiful. He smiled all the time. He was a curious baby, propped on my legs watching me. I was still falling in love while getting to know this amazing person.

Rebuilding my mental health took several doctors, a therapist, some meds, a Cognitive Behavioral Therapy program, a postpartum depression and anxiety moms' group, a husband and in-laws who went above and beyond taking over a lot of baby duties, calls from family and friends, and my mom and sister sharing their own experiences. Over a couple months, symptoms gradually started disappearing. I could sleep and breathe and enjoy the day. I don't know why this happened to me, what combination of hormones or genetics influenced the condition. But I did have joy all around me, especially from the sweet baby in my arms. I learned to let things go and not expect perfection. I allowed myself to be sad that I didn't have the experience of my dreams.

On a sunny, warm day in late March, I put on the Baby Bjorn, nestled T into the carrier so we were chest to chest, and took a walk through the neighborhood. He was almost three months old, and I was going back to work soon. I kissed the top of his head and started our blissful day.

In Clover

by TAMMY ROSE

My mother was lucky. She could find a four-leaf clover in a giant meadow or a tiny strip of green between a dirty sidewalk and a busy street. It was her secret superpower. Walking in a field, sure. Our backyard, of course. She'd find them when we were pulled over on the road, trying to take a break from vacation traffic. I find the ones she found and saved, pressed into books or in a Post-it pad. They were so commonplace to her that they'd be poking out of every stack of paper. Now that she's dead, they're her way of sending her luck to me.

We had both been lucky for a time when I was a child. In the years my father was alive, everything seemed sunny and fair weather. I was an only child, easy enough, a bookworm from an early age. Saturdays full of grocery shopping at the biggest supermarket downtown, then Lawrence Welk and the three of us curled up on the couch together. Normal family fights would end in laughter. Happily dull even for a sitcom.

Then he got sick with one of those mysterious illnesses that turn out to be several things going wrong at once. When you are in the hospital too long, it will eventually kill you. My mother spent the last month of his life sitting by his bed, holding his hand.

When he died, it seemed as if we had fallen out of grace with the Universe. We fell out of favor, falling into a hole of depression. She, much too young to be a widow; me, only eleven, suddenly a grown-up. We tried to hide our grief from each other, but she spent too long in the basement, crying by the washing machine, and I heard her. We switched places between parent and child a lot then. It would happen again a lifetime later, when she ended up in the hospital.

She was lucky. Her whole last year on Earth, she was ready to go. After a full life, eighty years here, she was done. She kept saying that all she wanted was a new body. She was devoutly Roman Catholic, but her actual beliefs transcended her traditional theology. She embraced reincarnation and the Concordian Transcendental ideas of living in harmony with the divine in Mother Nature.

When the doctors determined there was nothing more to do, she was ready. Her doctors were surprised; most people want every last effort until the body wears out. Nope; just find her a quiet room. All she wanted was quiet at the end.

So I sat vigil with her, holding her hand during her final week in the hospital. In the same way she had sat by my father's bedside at my age. As much as I had been determined not to be overwhelmed like we had been by my father's death, it took me by surprise.

I tried to be with her every moment, even when all I had was her breath. After listening carefully, I could tell when that changed too. I watched her final breaths, her chest rising and falling. When everything was still, when I expected to feel the deepest loss of my life, I suddenly felt elation, as if her spirit had been set free from the pain of this world, like it had taken off like a bird, had risen, had left behind gravity and pain and memories and was now free. What I sensed was her release—the opposite of falling.

Since then, of course, I have fallen into a strangely familiar grief: having to face the sheer audacity that I have to live in a world where her wonderful presence is absent. I've again fallen out of favor of the Universe, and nothing is right or possible without her. But I have our house and the layers of our years here together, both the good years and the awful moments. And I find another four-leaf clover hidden in a mystery book or on her nightstand. I won't always be this fallen woman, weighed down with grief and loss. I think of the ups and downs of my mother's life, and I smile. We did it together. If she could do it, I can do it.

The Couch Story

by EMILY RAYMOND

I never knew my grandmother, Emmeline Streigle. Born Emmeline Albano in 1912, she died at the age of seventy-eight, two years before I was born. However, in her absence, I had stories of a remarkable woman. She was born to Italian immigrants, her father a cobbler and her mother a housewife, fondly remembered as a perpetually smiling, small, round woman who stood over the stove stirring a pot of sauce. My grandmother was raised speaking Italian and as a result was held back her first year of school for not knowing enough English. Nevertheless, Emmeline was intelligent, hardworking, and while sometimes a bit slow on the uptake (often laughing at a joke several minutes after everyone else), she had a passion for science. A small woman, she would lie about her height, telling people she was four-foot-eleven and three-quarters because "five feet was too far to go." After graduating from high school, she convinced her father to send her to college. She was the only one of his four children to do so. In 1932 she enrolled in the then Connecticut Agricultural College, which changed its name a few years later to the University of Connecticut (UConn).

Being Pre-Med wasn't easy for a woman in 1932. The only place, for example, to get urine for lab work was the men's bathroom, and Emmeline had to rely on her friends for the necessary supplies. Still, despite the institutional obstacles, Emmeline graduated with a Bachelor of Science in Chemistry and Bacteriology in 1937. Starting off doing clinical lab work at Waterbury Hospital, she later worked at New Britain General Hospital, eventually becoming chief technician in the 1940s. It was there she met my grandfather John, and they married after the war. After a while, it seemed that children would not be in her future, so she decided to leave the hospital and open a private lab with her best friend and fellow hospital technician Lucia. They borrowed $1,500 from Lucia's father and began to set up their new business. They found an office, purchased lab equipment, and procured insurance through Lloyds of London, as no American insurance firm would assume the risk of two women running a medical lab. Once those details were settled, the two women set out to buy office furniture.

It was winter in the '90s, and Emmeline and Lucia decided to make a day of it. They put on their finest clothes, including their Persian lamb coats, and set out. They had a tight budget and needed a couch for patients to lie down on during a timed test. While perusing the selection of sofas at a furniture store, a salesman approached who asked if he could help them with anything. My grandmother replied, "Oh, it doesn't have to be good; we only need it a half hour at a time." The salesman's jaw dropped, much to Emmeline's bewilderment and Lucia's laughter. The salesman had assumed that these two ladies in elegant coats were in fact ladies of the night! This small, four-foot-nine Italian woman had blatantly told him they were couch shopping for a couch to ply their scandalous trade! The moment of course passed, the two women found a couch to suit their needs, and the Community Clinical Laboratory began operation as the first lab of its kind in New Britain. It was the only one owned and operated by women. Emmeline, that fierce, briefly fallen woman, would pass on her stories of ferocity, fearlessness, and obliviousness to her daughter; her daughter, who would become my mother, could then pass them along to me.

The Gift

by MIA YANOSY

I know the meanings of lots of names. This is what I told Michael when we met for the first time. Much to my surprise, he did not seem to think I was odd when I told him that Charles means "free man" or that Amelia means "work." We walked to a little pizza place down the street from my house for our first date. It went well.

One reason I like names so much is because I was named for my own grandmother, who was called Angela, but also Nonna, which means "grandmother" in Italian. Angela means "angel," and when she died, people said she was one.

Nonna was warm and generous, but also sensible and tough. She survived cancer and multiple strokes and all of her own family. She cooked meatballs from memory, eyeing the breadcrumbs and seasonings. She always coughed after eating ice cream. She loved thriller novels. She hated the heat. If it's there, you can have it, she'd say whenever I'd ask to take a soda from the fridge.

Michael and I went on our second date the day after she went to the hospital. She'd had a headache, and finally decided to let my mother take her to the emergency room. Michael and I went to three different hamburger chains and played arcade games, and I tried to field the texts coming in.

At the hospital, the doctors confirmed that Nonna had a brain bleed and would need surgery. Michael could attest now that I was not concerned. She had survived so much, and she was not at all ready to go. She still cooked and cleaned and babysat my young cousins. Ten days later, she died.

I was a late bloomer when it came to dating and sex. Michael was first, in almost every sense of the word. He gave me beautiful compliments and made me laugh. He felt deeply. Best of all, I knew, in every cell of my body, that I could trust him.

The first time I went to his house, I stayed late. Kissing was still new to me, addictive, and made me feel like a different person. My mother called me several times that evening before I realized, around 1:00 a.m.

When I called her back, she asked, "When are you coming home?"

I said, "I don't know. I am an adult. Don't ruin this for me."

Her voice was pained when she told me she was worried about Nonna.

I didn't realize how bad things were when I was with Michael. In fact, nothing felt very bad for weeks, even after Nonna died, because I was falling in love with him. I cried a lot after Nonna's death, but mostly I felt shocked, and I still wanted to see Michael every moment I could.

I wasn't sure if I should be ashamed that my grief wasn't big enough. Sad enough. During the months after her death, I wasn't sure how feelings worked at all—how two could exist at once, or how one could completely overpower the other. I wondered how awful grief had to be so that even love couldn't make it go away.

I was raised Catholic, but my relationship with God is almost non-existent. Still, sometimes I think there must be something like a God to make things like this happen. How is it that I found Michael right as I lost my Nonna? Who sent him? Who gave him to me?

One meaning of Michael is "gift from God."

Despite what I believe about God, I am certain that falling in love with Michael made it easier to lose Nonna. I don't know if this is right or wrong. When Nonna died, it seemed like a vacuum appeared, ready to suck down all of the love I had for her. Instead, I held that love tight to my body, and every time I saw Michael, I let go.

Nursery Rhymes

by JOAN MULLER

At three years old, I befriended a solitary apple tree next door in an un-mowed acre behind my grandmother's house. Like it, I was feral and an only child. Climbing in the lowest crooks of the ancient tree seemed like my birthright. If my shyness duped my parents into expecting my good behavior when they weren't looking, my Memere demanded I get down NOW because I was GOING TO FALL. While I had figured out that if I slipped it would my fault, hers seemed a faithless claim beyond that, more like I was *faulty*, doomed by astrology, born in the house of probable cause. *Rock-a-bye, baby.*

I kept climbing anyway, figuring that more skill and stealth would diminish guilt. I saw real improvement over a couple of birthdays. Then discovery! The ultimate way to evade adult surveillance was to perform my own reconnaissance from the tree's concealing crown. I was all in for the long game now. *On the treetop.*

At eight, after my family relocated to a brand new 1950s subdivision, I discovered a large stand of white pines an easy bike ride away. There, undisturbed, I climbed higher than ever before or read aloud to my coniferous audience, keeping pilfered Lestoil on hand to remove sap stains that would require explanation at home later. *When the wind blows.*

One day that summer, a young man from the neighborhood interrupted my reading with a casualness that quickly became capture. Impossible to fight, he hauled me—disembodied as a window-stunned bird—into thick brush beyond the grove. "Don't you tell!" he threatened. *The cradle will rock.*

After he left, I slowly coalesced, reviving—there were my strewn clothes, my little inside-out socks tossed aside. Two things became clear: He knew what he had done was wrong, and now so did I. You bet I would tell my mom, if only to ensure the trees' innocence. *When the bough breaks.*

My wracked mother explained how things could happen to girls—things Memere didn't hint of. She desperately rebuked how I shouldn't have been there, but it didn't matter anymore. This was a game changer worse than falling; disaster hadn't come from climbing trees after all, but from fated moments when I had not been up in one. Here was shame beyond Memere or cleansing, nowhere to hide anymore. *The cradle will fall.*

The assailant's family sent him across the country to relatives. I assume Mom had had strong words with someone, prompting this, but it remained just our secret. Then it became like it never happened. *And down will come baby, cradle and all.*

Forty years later, I was a married teacher in a village in a different state, tending my apple trees and scores of students. I championed all of them to reach high for what they thought was beyond their grasp, fingers crossed for their good harvest. My heartwood felt intact despite how my twig had been bent.

It shattered our staff when a student's father I had never met was arrested for felony counts of child pornography and assault. Facts about the minors were confidential, but national wire services networked news about him and prompted an old friend from grade school to call me long-distance. She quipped that some given names must be cursed. How else to explain how the abuser she had just learned about near me had the same name as the disruptive fellow who had been in her older brother's class before suddenly dropping out of school? Ridiculous, we said. Coincidence, I hoped.

Yet coincidence wasn't done with me yet. A recycled newspaper beneath muddy boots in my classroom seized my attention a few weeks later with a headline naming our school. I read information I already knew, the offender's name—that old preposterousness—but then came his bio, including hometown and age, the other shoe dropping. Here was the real dirt.

Forty years of my moot grievance had lived in silence, but my neglected voice, once provoked, cleared its throat. As if restoring lost childhood habits, I went out on a limb, contacting the district victims' advocate. My claim for justice had expired, but my bearing witness to it again could demonstrate the longevity of the accused's serial offenses, which would affect sentencing. This might connect a story to its origin by an unimaginable time and space trajectory, but truth has no "best used by" date. Some who have fallen can still take a stand, dear Memere. So grows the tree.

Emerald Shoes

by EMMA CORBY

After the ultimatum, my relationship had thirteen months left. Thirteen months of happy-ish days and half-happy nights. Thirteen months with a foundation of doubt and hesitancy, built up from unsteady rocks of silence and ignorance. Fifty-seven weeks of never knowing whether my smile was real. I continued to fall for what I'd agreed on: everything.

Because it was everything or nothing, and nothing scared me. Everything didn't seem scary because it led somewhere; everything had a future. Nothing led to nowhere, and that's where I had already been. I was surrounded by nothing, and never knew how free I was.

But I didn't want everything yet. Agreeing to everything gave directions to the future, and I wanted to pick my turns as they came; I didn't want to follow a map. But I wanted that destination. I wanted that future. And at the time, having to make life decisions around one man scared me less than making life decisions aimlessly. I was willing to take the choice out of my choices so I wouldn't be alone—I fell for it.

And for the next thirteen months, I ignored the half-hearted greetings from the couch in the other room every time I visited. I ignored the silence that hovered over every table we ate at, my apologies filling the empty air with no reasoning behind them, just feeling sorry for taking up space. I ignored the blurs in my mind every time I tried to imagine a future with him. I was pretending to feel loved, and he was pretending to love. Too bad for me, it wasn't the other way around.

I slept with sighs every night; he made me out to be unlovable, when really, he couldn't love me. He couldn't see the way I organized his closet when he was gone, or the way I made sure his fridge had more than just beer and mustard in it. To him there was never dust, because it never showed up in the first place. His pillowcases were never twisted because they simply stayed straight. Keeping his shoes on the doormat and his keys on the hook above the light switch became my afternoons' concerns; it never occurred to me that I didn't even have a place to hang my coat.

Now I realize that, really, it was too bad for him.

Thirteen months and zero fights later, I fell deeper into the emptiness I constantly felt in my chest and, on the way down, realized I had been alone the whole time. I could feel its entire weight without wiping somebody else's toothpaste from the sink. And I was wonderfully sad. I could go to bed whenever I wanted, didn't have to apologize for taking up a cushion on a couch or wait until the hockey game was between halves to talk—or quarters, thirds, periods . . . whatever hockey is separated into.

I am not afraid of eye contact anymore. I can look somebody in the eyes, and when they look back at me, I no longer flit my gaze to the ground in fear of being looked through. I no longer go to bed with somebody facing the other way, falling asleep before a "goodnight." There are no more showers taken before me, without asking if I need them first. I don't sit at silent dinners anymore. I've learned to laugh with my eyes crinkling and, when I laugh hard enough, to snort.

I fell into the stereotype of a man giving a woman an ultimatum, and, even worse, I fell for the ultimatum—the ultimatum with no room for snort laughing. Thankfully, I was pushed off the rocks.

And if I ever do get another relationship ultimatum, I am gassing up the Subaru Outback and driving away like my twenty-four-year-old brother drives his cherry-red Mustang. And I suggest you do the same; you don't need to know my brother to know how he drives. Get the hell out of there. I don't care if it's given over a paid all-you-can-eat sushi buffet or engraved in emerald shoes. . . . Floor it.

Rebel Pants

by AMY MULLIS

"Can you operate a ten-key calculator?"

"Yes!" Mom looked the manager in the eye—and promptly signed up for a business class to learn how.

She had her eye on a position as a bookkeeper in the days when other moms baked cupcakes for class parties and whipped up clever casseroles for dinner. Mom baked her share of cupcakes, sewed my clothes, and made biscuits from scratch, but if there was a shortcut to get dinner on the table, she was the first to try it. She had other things to do.

She was a Southern lady to be sure; maybe not the kind who wore pearls and Elizabeth Arden makeup on her day off, but the kind who would slip somebody a dollar if they didn't have enough money at the cash register.

She believed knowledge led to good choices. She exposed us kids to all kinds of music, from country to classical, to books—I didn't know about censorship until I learned in high school that I had already read many of the titles on the banned books list—and to theater. Anything that would broaden our experience as human beings.

Back in the days when Mayberry morals ruled the airwaves and Andy Griffith was the next best thing to a thirteenth disciple, Mama took us to church just as any devoted mother in the Red Mud section of the South would do.

But Mama did not like hats. And ladies wore hats to church. It was part of the uniform. So, she wore hats.

Except one sparkling Sunday morning, when she didn't.

I was pretty sure the no-hat thing counted as one of the Seven Deadly Sins. But Mom made her own choices, using a bizarre strategy she called common sense. Small-town churches in the 1960s didn't use common sense for their dress codes. They used tradition, and tradition is not a creative fashion designer.

Soon, I heard around the neighborhood that Mama was that most dangerous of things—a rebel. But I noticed a bareheaded trend in church after that. Maybe the ladies of the Charter Members Bible Class just needed someone to lead the charge.

So one winter morning a decade or so later, when the mercury in the thermometer would have to do push-ups to reach above the mid-20s, Mama said it would be okay to wear pants to church. I slid a pair of warm slacks over my shivering legs. I was a shy teenager, but frost has a way of dimming self-consciousness.

There weren't as many hats in the crowd as there used to be before Mom staged her rebellion, but there weren't any pantsuits either. No Capri pants, no leggings, definitely no jeans. It was socially acceptable for your miniskirt to stir up an ill wind, but marching through the First Baptist Church sanctuary in slacks was a stroll down the Highway to Hell.

I paused in the doorway to the sanctuary. Behind me, the door that led to escape routes through the Sunday school wing snapped shut with a click. No turning back now. Three hundred well-bred faces looked up at me, and time stopped.

In ancient Rome, the common solution for weeding out trouble-makers, rowdies, and hooligans who wore trousers to church was to have them for dinner at the Colosseum. All things considered, that seemed like a kinder, gentler fate than parting the pews with an outfit sure to set the lion's share of tongues wagging before lunchtime.

My face felt hot enough to melt the icicles outside the windows, but nothing could defrost the looks I was getting inside. Life lessons are often painful to swallow and harder to digest, but as I paused, looking out over the congregation that day, light fought through the stained glass, and I realized a truth that turned out to be far more important than the dress code for a church service.

My mama wasn't only a rebel. She was a teacher. If I could survive this fall from the stony wall of small-town grace, I could trust myself to make my own choices, to pave my own way, to walk my own path.

I took a deep breath and grinned at the ladies leaning over paunchy husbands to get a good look as I strolled to my seat and settled in for the sermon.

If Mama was a teacher, I was going to be the best student ever.

Because I'm my mama's daughter.

And a rebel.

Acknowledgments

Without David LeGere and the gang at Woodhall, there would be no *Fast Fallen Women*—at least not between two covers—of a book.

The *Fast Women* series began over coffee in my University of Connecticut (UConn) office in the spring of 2019. My office is the one with the decorated door in the basement, right next to the vending machine and the restroom. It was the same office Dave used to visit when he was my creative writing student. In 2019, Dave showed up to my door, newly minted as CEO of Woodhall Press, with coffee and an invitation to create a collection of original works by prominent and emerging women writers.

Thank you to Margaret Moore at Woodhall for her ingenuity and her wise support. Thanks also to Laura Rossi, as always, for her help in getting the book into the hands of readers.

Thank you to all the writers in *Fast Funny Women, Fast Fierce Women,* and in *Fast Fallen Women* for making us gasp, laugh, weep, hug, and realize that we're not crazy—and that we're not alone.

I owe wild thanks to Nicole Catarino, also a UConn graduate, now on her way to graduate degrees elsewhere, who has been a contributor to all three volumes. Her writing is impressive, of course, but it does not give anyone a true glimpse of the work she's done on behalf of the series. Nicole wrangled authors and agents, edited pieces by emerging and seasoned authors, proofread, copyedited, secured bios and photos (getting writers to send images of themselves is like getting members of the Mob to send family photos) and reminded me that I had to answer that email today.

Nicole's predecessor, Julia Marrinan (a contributor to *Fast Fierce Women*), had taught her well. I continue to owe Julia thanks.

Following in their impossible footsteps are Alexander Grant and Claire Lasher, more recent inhabitants of my ground-floor English office. Alex and Claire have kept this most current volume on track and me on task. They demanded I rewrite the introduction, which it needed. With their own insights, intelligence, and indefatigable wit they made *Fast Fallen Women* the gem that it is. Claire's essay is one of the highlights of this book.

UConn, where I have taught since 1987, has supported these books in myriad ways, both directly and indirectly. When it's come to *Fallen*, they've really stepped up.

To my husband, my beloved Michael Meyer—writer, editor, and anthologist extraordinaire—with love and gratitude. There is no quiz. Here's to falling and rising, arm in arm.

About the Contributors

Kelly Andrews-Babcock lives in the Quiet Corner of northeastern Connecticut. She's been a member of the Church of Springsteen for about forty years. When she's not chasing Bruce, she's busy teaching, reading, gardening, or walking the dogs in the woods.

Anne Bagamery is a journalist based in Paris. She grew up in the Detroit suburbs and graduated in 1978 from Dartmouth, where she was the first female editor in chief of *The Dartmouth* campus daily. A former senior editor of the late, lamented *International Herald Tribune* in Paris, her work has appeared in *Forbes, Institutional Investor, Savvy, Worth,* the *International New York Times,* Vogue.com, *The American Lawyer,* and *Persuasion.* Her essay "Clean Copy" appeared in *Fast Fierce Women.*

Louisa Ballhaus is an New York City–based writer and editor with work in *Betches, Bustle, She-Knows,* and *Merry Jane.* She worked on HBO Max's *Search Party* and was the poetry editor for literary magazine *2 Bridges Review.* Her poetry has appeared in *Free State Review.* Louisa earned her BA in English from Wesleyan University.

I'm **Ilene Beckerman**, and I'm supposed to write a bio here.

Are they kidding? I'm eighty-seven years old—I'll need at least eighty-seven pages, not including footnotes. I'd like to focus on my life, maybe starting with how I lost my virginity at the Dartmouth Winter Carnival in 1954, but maybe that's not appropriate.

Anyway, I wrote five books. You can check out my website: IleneBeckerman.com. Not as interesting as that night in 1954. For details, email me at gingyib@comcast.net.

Originally from Chicago, **Pia Bertucci** relocated to the Carolinas to pursue a doctorate in Italian from the University of North Carolina at Chapel Hill. Currently, she is the Director of Italian at the University of South Carolina.

In addition to her 2015 novel, *Between Milk and India*, Pia has published on Italian women writers, Italian food studies, and the Italian language. When she's not working, Pia can be found eating her way through Italy, soaking in the Colorado hot springs, attending Toad the Wet Sprocket concerts, or enjoying time with her husband, four children, and two dogs.

Angela Bonavoglia is the author of *Good Catholic Girls: How Women Are Leading the Fight to Change the Church*. Her first book, *The Choices We Made: 25 Women and Men Speak Out About Abortion* (foreword by Gloria Steinem), featured her interviews with celebrities, writers, activists, clerics, and medical providers about their experiences with abortion (1920s–1980s). Her work has appeared in many venues, including *Ms.* (longtime contributing editor), *The Nation*, the *Chicago Tribune, Religion Dispatches, Women's Media Center, Rewire, Huff-Post,* and various collections, most recently, her essay "Blindsided" in *Poets and Writers on Sexual Assault*.

Erin Brochu, University of Connecticut (Class of 2021), earned a Bachelor of Arts in English and a Bachelor of Arts in Music. She is pursuing her passion through a Masters of Music in Vocal Performance with a concentration in Musical Theatre at NYU Steinhardt. When she's not singing or writing, Erin freelances as a hand-lettering artist and enjoys film photography. She is honored to be recognized by her inimitable English Professor, Dr. Barreca, by being included in this book and is thrilled to be featured among such an incredible group of fast fallen women!

Erica Buehler is a writer and editor you'll find at the intersection of food, travel, and all things that make the heart sing. She's based in Denver, Colorado, but hopes to see every corner of the world someday, an adventure that will be fueled by coffee, the oxygen her houseplants provide, and literal puppy love from her dog, Peanut. Erica has written for *Fast Funny Women, Thrillist, Livability, Out Front* magazine, *Mashed*, and several other publications.

Michelle P. Carter is a sex-positive, sex-averse, panromantic gray-asexual. And, yes, what a mouthful for someone who never has her mouth full of anything but bacon mac and cheese and fresh *nigiri*. A content creator with more than 100,000 followers, 3M+ likes, and 15.3M+ views under the moniker AsexualMemes, Michelle hopes to educate, inspire, and make you laugh with her queer content. Because figuring out your sexuality is hard enough. Why not laugh about it? And, indeed, isn't that the whole vibe of this anthology?

Cristina Cabral Caruk was born in Portugal and immigrated to the United States as an infant. She is a graduate of West Conn (Class of 1988) and the University of Connecticut School of Law (Class of 1991), is barred in Connecticut and New York, and worked as a civil litigation lawyer for more than twenty years. Since 2015 she has worked in the insurance industry full-time as an attorney auditor. Her first published work was a shorty story of fiction titled "Christmas Comes Early," which appeared in the anthology *Joseph, You Take The Baby*. She lives in Connecticut. As of this writing, her daughter is pregnant with Cristina's first grandchild.

Nicole Catarino is a poet, translator, and writer born and raised in Connecticut. She graduated from the University of Connecticut with a BA in English and a minor in literary translations in 2022. Her writing has appeared in the *Hartford Courant*, *New Square Journal*, *Long River Review*, and *Women's Media Center*, and she was also a contributor and editor for the previous *Fast Women* anthologies: *Fast Funny Women* and *Fast Fierce Women*. If everything goes according to plan, she is currently working toward her master's in Library and Information Science. If not, she's definitely still writing.

 **Jane Cook** is a lifelong learner who has worked as an educator for nearly fifty years. She has worked part-time with the Connecticut Writing Project at the University of Connecticut since 2007. This picture is from the era when her piece occurred, with her beloved horse, Trisha, whom she rescued at age eighteen. When Trisha died at age thirty-four, Jane had never fallen off her. When not working, Jane spends her time rescuing animals and paying veterinary bills. Jane lives in Mansfield Center, Connecticut, with her husband and current animal family members: Zen, Willow, Joy, and Ami.

"Have laptop, will write." **Barbara Cooley** is a former college instructor and nonprofit administrator and consultant who now writes for the sheer pleasure of it. Her current projects include the story of her brother's fierce battle with leukemia and an epic narrative detailing five generations of one line in her family that mirrors the story of America. She lives in her happy place along the Lake Michigan shoreline with her husband and her rescue dog, who believes *he* is her only laptop. Her other talents of note include cherry-pit spitting and eight ball pool, although no calls her Eight Ball anymore.

 **Emma Corby** grew up in Rochester, New York, with her wonderfully chaotic family of six. After working for her family's dairy and swimming competitively, she attended the University of Connecticut, where she swam Division One while also rediscovering her love for reading. Emma graduated from UConn with a degree in English, with at least five of Gina's classes on her transcript. Now, based on a simple "What if I moved to Alaska?" thought, she's at the University of Alaska Fairbanks as both a teaching assistant and a grad student, graduating with a Master of Arts degree in English in 2023.

Susan Cossette lives and writes in Minneapolis, Minnesota. The author of *Peggy Sue Messed Up*, she is a recipient of the University of Connecticut's Wallace Stevens Poetry Prize. A two-time Pushcart Prize nominee, look for her work in *Rust and Moth*, *ONE ART*, *As It Ought to Be, Anti-Heroin Chic, The Amethyst Review, Crow & Cross Keys, Loch Raven Review*, and in the anthologies *Tuesdays at Curley's* and *After the Equinox*. She is Director of Annual Giving at a prep school but secretly wishes she was a member of the English department. Be sure to ask about her cats, Sylvia and Chuck.

Julie Danis is a writer, storyteller, and former global marketing/advertising executive. As a business humorist, she wrote a *Chicago Tribune* column called "It's a Living" and contributed commentary to Marketplace radio. She was a writer for the award-winning documentary film *The Girl Who Wore Freedom* and has been published in the 2022 anthology *Storyteller's True Stories About Love, Huffington Post, More,* and *Life Reimagined.* Julie was an adjunct lecturer at Northwestern University and is a graduate of the Second City School of Improvisation. Her favorite professional title was Director of Mind & Mood.

Marna Deitch is an interpreter for the deaf, certified motorcycle instructor, wedding officiant, Advisory Board member for the City of West Hollywood, and an actor. She attended State University of New York at Oswego in upstate New York, where she studied Theatre and Industrial/Organization Psychology, which enabled her to be the best darn bartender around. She is happy and proud if her story has helped or motivated anyone to understand that pain might be devastating, but we never know what wonderful places it might lead us to.

Lisa Douglas is an author and playwright from Connecticut. She holds BAs in English and Theatre Studies from the University of Connecticut, as well as an MFA in Playwriting from Columbia University. She is the most treasured (only) aunt of Chamyra, Alvin, and Simone; the best-loved (again, only) sister of Gregory and Alvin; the ultimately adored (she has no others) sister-in-law of Heather; and the absolute favorite (you guessed it, only) daughter of Alvin and Marjorie.

Cindy Eastman is an award-winning author whose first book, *Flip-Flops After 50: And Other Thoughts on Aging I Remembered to Write Down*, is a collection of humorous essays on getting older. She is the creator of the "Writual" writing program and has presented nationally at the Story Circle Network Women's Writing Conference. She is a contributor to several anthologies published by the University of Dayton's Erma Bombeck Writers' Workshop, Woodhall Press, and She Writes Press. She writes more about aging in a weekly newsletter called *Silver Linings* and teaches English at Naugatuck Community College.

Bonnie Jean Feldkamp is the opinion editor for the Pulitzer Prize–winning *Louisville Courier Journal*. She is also a syndicated columnist with Creators Syndicate. Bonnie Jean lives with her family in Louisville, Kentucky. Find her on social media (@WriterBonnie) or at WriterBonnie.com.

Jennifer Forrest was originally inspired by Gina Barecca while attending her creative writing classes at the University of Connecticut. In 2020, she left her twenty-year retail career, where she was a fearless business leader who had a passion for building teams and delivering results. She is now on her new path, discovering her next chapter. Jennifer has prior work featured in *Fast Fierce Women*. She is an avid reader, amateur gardener and enthusiastic baker. She resides in Connecticut with her husband, their three boys, and a menagerie of pets.

Darien Hsu Gee is the best-selling author of five novels published by Penguin Random House that have been translated into eleven languages. Her collection of micro essays, *Allegiance*, received the 2021 Bronze IPPY award in the Essays category. Darien is the recipient of a 2019 Poetry Society of America's Chapbook Fellowship award for *Other Small Histories* and the 2015 Hawai'i Book Publishers' Ka Palapala Po'okela Award of Excellence for *Writing the Hawai'i Memoir*, as well as a Sustainable Arts Foundation grant and a Vermont Studio Center fellowship. She lives with her family on the Big Island of Hawai'i.

Carol Gieg graduated from Dartmouth College and earned a master's degree in Social Welfare and Public Health from the University of California, Berkeley.

Carol suffered a brain injury but returned to work three months after neurosurgery and continued working ten years before retiring. Her memoir, *TBI—To Be Injured: Surviving and Thriving After a Brain Injury*, has been recommended by victims, their loved ones, neurologists, and writers. It is available through Amazon and tbitobeinjured.com.

Carol's poetry and prose have been published in anthologies and presented through various forms of public media. She lives in Benicia, California, with her husband, Luis, who has dementia. Her next book, *Dementia: A Handbook for Caregivers*, is based on her experience as a caregiver.

Cecilia Gigliotti is a New England–born writer, photographer, podcaster, and musician based in Berlin, Germany. She holds an MA in English Literature from Central Connecticut State University and a BA in Creative Writing from the Writers Institute at Susquehanna University. She serves as editor in chief of the *Women*Writing Berlin Lab* magazine (wearewwbl. com). Her short fiction, nonfiction, poetry, and art have appeared in numerous collections, anthologies, journals, and newspapers, including Woodhall Press's *Flash Nonfiction Food* (2020).

Rosie Speedlin Gonzalez is the presiding judge of Bexar County Court at Law No. 13 and REFLEJO COURT, a treatment court for first-time offenders of family violence. She has received the Judge John C. Creuzot Award for Judicial Vision & Leadership "For Courage, Vision and Conviction in the Justice System" and the Texas Diversity Council's LGBTQ+ Individual Leadership Award. Judge Gonzalez has received the Alice Wright Franzke Feminist Award for outstanding work she has done—and will continue to do—that promotes the ideals of peace, empowerment, cooperation, equality, and respect of all persons.

Kim A. Hanson is an award-winning, retired business communicator who received her BS in English literature from Fairfield University. She has written for the *New York Times, Connecticut Magazine*, the *Examiner* website, and industry magazines. Prior to her retirement, she held directorships within various Fortune 200 corporations and ran her own successful consulting practice for fourteen years.

Kim lives within walking distance of the shoreline in Rhode Island with her husband, Tom, and their maniacal rescue hound, Brandy, who believes that all freelance writing time should be spent throwing a tennis ball. Kim has many more short stories to write.

Emily Heiden's writing has been published in the *Washington Post, Lit Hub, Electric Literature*, the *Seattle Times*, the *Hartford Courant, Brevity* magazine, *Colorado Review*, and elsewhere. She has also spoken about reproductive rights on NPR. In addition to this anthology, her essays have been published in the books *Don't Look Now: Things We Wish We Hadn't Seen* (Ohio State University Press) and *Fast Funny Women: 75 Essays of Flash Nonfiction*, also from Woodhall Press.

Emily holds a PhD in Creative Writing and Literature from the University of Cincinnati and an MFA in Creative Nonfiction from George Mason University.

Monique Heller was born and raised in Essex, Connecticut. She came out of the womb funny and is "that friend" who must be told to behave herself in "classy settings." She became known for creating the "Joebituary" and putting the "fun" in funeral. After her piece was published in Gina's compilation *Fast Funny Women*, she was subsequently asked, "Fast How?" and "How Fast?" by many far and wide. She attempts to mother two teen/tween-age girls and hopes to inspire them to look at life through a different lens.

Jianna Heuer is a psychotherapist in private practice in New York City. She holds a Bachelor of Arts in Psychology and English from the University of Connecticut and started her professional life working in book publishing and freelance writing. Always passionate about social justice issues, the publishing industry did not satisfy her craving to help people in their everyday lives. In 2008 Jianna went back to school, and in 2011 she completed her master's in Social Work at New York University. Throughout her career shifts and now, she continues to write.

Katherine Jimenez is a senior at the University of Connecticut, studying journalism and English with a concentration in Creative Writing. She is a former opinion columnist for the *Daily Campus*, UConn's student newspaper, and has worked with Connecticut Public Radio as a freelance social media manager. She is the first English major to be awarded a BOLD Scholarship at UConn, choosing to write a novel that focuses on mother-daughter relationships in Latin America for her project. When she isn't thinking about what story to write about next, you can probably find her at a bookstore.

Melissa Babcock Johnson holds an MFA in Creative and Professional Writing from Western Connecticut State University and a BA in English from the University of Connecticut. Originally from Springfield, Massachusetts, she grew up in East Haddam, Connecticut. Her career has revolved around newspapers and magazines along the Connecticut shoreline and recently expanded to include teaching writing and research to college students. She and her husband enjoy hosting exchange students, who come from all over the world to attend high school in the United States.

Angel Johnstone is an erotica author and sexuality and confidence coach for women. Her brand of female-centric erotica and her group coaching work help women by tapping into their most underutilized power source: desire. It is Angel's belief that women lead best when they can own their full power, and part of that power is their sexuality. Many women find themselves in midlife searching for that lost power, as they have "turned off" to get through the hectic days with kids, spouses, parents, and coworkers—all looking for support and nurturing. Women

who learn to turn passion back on and explore their deep desires, with wild abandon, she believes, are the ones thriving and leading the way.

Angel writes short stories, runs an online adult toy boutique, and teaches classes on pleasure, intimate connection, money mindset, and feminine confidence both in and out of the bedroom.

Katie Girard Jones graduated from the University of Connecticut in 1993, where she received the Robert Wooster Stallman Prize and was a finalist for the Chase Going Woodhouse Prize. She has taught high school, worked as an editor and copywriter, wrangled tourists, helped pilot an eighty-two-foot schooner across Long Island Sound, and paid off student loans for an unfinished graduate degree. She currently substitute teaches elementary school and lives in Mystic, Connecticut, with her husband, two sons, and beloved pit bull. Sometimes she writes.

Pamela Katz is a screenwriter most known for her work with legendary director Margarethe von Trotta, including *Hannah Arendt* (one of the *New York Times* critic A.O. Scott's Top Ten Films). As an author, she's published essays and articles, as well as *The Partnership: Brecht, Weill, Three Women, and Germany on the Brink* (Doubleday/Nan A. Talese). The *New Yorker* proclaimed: "Katz restores the women to their proper place in the story, with levity, strong characterization, and beguiling descriptions of interwar Germany crackling with politics, art and a sense of possibility."

Cara Erdheim Kilgallen is an associate professor of English at Sacred Heart University in Fairfield, Connecticut, where she has taught since 2010. A native New Yorker, she feels enlivened by the energy of urban living but also appreciates her time hiking in the mountains when she visits family every summer in southern Idaho. She is fortunate to have family and friends all over the United States and has studied abroad in England and Spain. Cara truly values the mind-body connection; she has passions for poetry, literature, writing, figure skating, tennis, and golf. She is extremely close to family and relishes her new role as a mother.

"Rituals of Resurgence" is her first deeply personal piece, and while some have cautioned against the potential stigma of exposing her battle with obsessive compulsive disorder, she feels strongly that attaching her name to this piece will inspire and empower others to persevere through life's hurdles. Cara hopes this essay will demonstrate that those with OCD can live happy, healthy, and productive lives without stigma or shame.

Dr. Misty L. Knight is a professor of Communication Studies and director of Women's and Gender Studies at Shippensburg University. She has been teaching courses and providing individual coaching in communication skills and public speaking for about twenty-five years. Her primary research interests involve activism, political rhetoric, self-defense rhetoric, and humor in communication. She teaches courses such as Gender and Communication, Public Speaking, Interpersonal Communication, and Political Rhetoric. She lives in Shippensburg with her teenage boys, of whom she is incredibly proud, and her furry babies.

Sarite Alterman Konier is an educator who took a detour into being a SAHM/Family Caregiver along the way. She has a BA in English with a concentration in Creative Writing from the University of Connecticut, as well as a California State K-8 Teaching Credential and Certificate in Day School Education from Hebrew Union College Los Angeles's DeLeT (Day School Leadership through Training) program. Now that her parts aren't falling out of her, she is focusing on her writing and career goals, and aims to return to a life committed to social justice and activism.

Claire Lasher graduated from the University of Connecticut with a BA in English in 2023. When not at school she can be found working for a family law firm on Cape Cod, which has proven to be a great place for developing empathy and acquiring an acute interest in stories that capture the turbulent nature of our everyday lives. She is currently pursuing family law at the University of Connecticut School of Law, but her greatest goal is to one day have only one dash light on at a time. She is incredibly grateful for all of the Fast Fallen Women in her life that have shown her how to get up—and do it all again.

Caroline Leavitt is the *New York Times* best-selling author of *Pictures of You, Is This Tomorrow, With or Without You*, and nine other novels. Her thirteenth novel, *Days of Wonder*, will be published by Algonquin Books in 2024. A New York Foundation of the Arts Fellow, she was also long-listed for the Maine Readers Prize and was first prize winner of the *Redbook* Young Writers Contest for a story that grew into her first novel. A finalist in the Sundance Screenwriters Lab, Caroline runs a column/blog for *Psychology Today* titled "Runs in the Family," writes for AARP's *The Ethel*, reviews books for *People* magazine, and teaches story structure for the UCLA Writers' Program and private clients.

Caroline is the co-founder of A Mighty Blaze and generally goes to every movie ever made, lives on chocolate and coffee, and reads four books at a time. She's married to music journalist Jeff Tamarkin, and they have a brilliant, funny, grown son. Visit her at carolineleavitt.com.

Melissa Llarena is an author and coach who helps moms use their imagination as a superpower to launch businesses and raise resilient kids. She has a podcast called *An Interview with Melissa Llarena*, where she helps curious souls go from imagining to living a bold life. Melissa's background includes a psychology degree from NYU, an MBA from the Tuck School of Business at Dartmouth; she also holds a Transformational Coaching Academy certificate.

Melissa is a native New Yorker who lives in Austin, Texas, with her husband and three sons (in that mix are identical twins). Follow her on Instagram: @ melissallarena.

Jessie Lubka is a graduate of the University of Connecticut (Class of 2017). She currently resides in Denver, Colorado, and works in the admissions office at Colorado School of Mines. She always loved writing but never knew how far it could take her until she was introduced to Gina Barreca. One semester of Gina's Creative Writing class transformed Jessie's life from small-time journaling to being a full-blown published author (a few times over). Jessie keeps a catalog of her personal essays on her blog, *Live a Lubey Life*. She hopes to continue writing until her fingers fall off.

Bobbie Ann Mason's first short stories were published in the *New Yorker* during the 1980s. Her first collection, *Shiloh and Other Stories*, won the PEN/Hemingway Award for first fiction and was nominated for the National Book Award, the PEN/Faulkner Award, and the National Book Critics Circle Award. She received an Arts and Letters Award for Literature from the American Academy of Arts and Letters. Her first novel, *In Country* (1985), about a teenager whose father died in Vietnam before she was born, is taught widely in classes and was made into a Norman Jewison film starring Bruce Willis and Emily Lloyd. She was raised on her family's dairy farm in western Kentucky, and her memoir, *Clear Springs*, was a finalist for the Pulitzer Prize.

Bobbie earned her BA in English at the University of Kentucky in 1962; her MA at Harper College, State University of Binghamton, in 1966; and her PhD at the University of Connecticut in 1972. She has written several novels and short-story collections. Her newest novel, *Dear Ann*, returns to the Vietnam War as the looming background of a love story in the turbulent 1960s.

Sydney Melocowsky divides her time behind the keyboard and in the green apron of your local barista. She lives in Connecticut, where she cares for her beloved albino hedgehog, Frosty. She enjoys using words to transform memories into stories and lives a little through the process.

Maggie Mitchell is the author of the novel *Pretty Is*, which the *New York Times* called "a stunning, multi-layered debut." Her short fiction has appeared in *New Ohio Review*, *American Literary Review*, *Green Mountains Review*, and elsewhere. She has been awarded fellowships at the Sewanee Writers' Conference, the Vermont Studio Center, and the Millay Colony for the Arts. She lives in Atlanta and teaches Victorian Literature and Creative Writing at the University of West Georgia.

Honor Moore is author of *Our Revolution: A Mother and Daughter at Midcentury*, and her previous memoir, *The Bishop's Daughter*, was a finalist for the National Book Critics Circle Award and a *Los Angeles Times* Favorite Book of the Year. Her work has appeared in the *New Yorker*, the *Paris Review*, and the *American Scholar*. When still in her twenties, *Mourning Pictures*, Moore's play in verse about her mother's death, was produced on Broadway. *The White Blackbird, A Life of the Painter Margarett Sargent by Her Granddaughter* was a *New York Times* Notable Book. She lives and writes in New York, where she is on the faculty of The New School.

Joan Muller is a lifelong artist, horsewoman, and naturalist mesmerized by language. She has pursued her interests, believing that their combination is more than the sum of their parts: visual arts and gifted teacher (2002 Connecticut Teacher of the Year); book arts craftswoman; Hampton Writing Workshop founder; dressage working student; award-winning fine artist; and off-grid sustainable farmer with a side gig as wildlife rehabilitator. Joan received her BFA from The Hartford Art School and master's equivalent from the University of New Hampshire and Rhode Island School of Design. She is retired and now at the mercy of her muses full-time.

When **Amy Mullis** was three, she got in trouble for writing on the walls. At sixteen she won statewide honors writing humorous features for her high school newspaper. In college she majored in Literature and wrote long, involved essays on William Faulkner and was named English Major of the Year. For unknown reasons, this path led to a twenty-year stint as a part-time church secretary—a job made all the more difficult because you're not supposed to swear between 9: 00 a.m. and 3:00 p.m. Now retired, she's searching for a hobby that isn't deadly. Skydiving and knitting are already ruled out.

Brenda Murphy is the author of more than twenty books, mostly about American drama and theater. Recently she has been writing biography, memoir, and biographical fiction. Her latest books include *Becoming Carlotta: A Biographical Novel* (2019), based on the life of the actress Carlotta Monterey; *Eugene O'Neill Remembered* (2017), a biography in documents; and *After the Voyage: An Irish American Story* (2016), historical fiction based on her immigrant family. She is currently obsessed with a novel set during the Salem witch trials.

Ebony Murphy-Root joined the English faculty of Saint Ann's School in Brooklyn in 2022 and serves on the boards of Arts Alive, which provides a creative platform for educational training to young people through music and performing arts, and the Independent Shakespeare Company. Ebony, a University of Connecticut alumna, is passionate about community and civic engagement and supporting the literary and cultural arts.

Pat Myers was the "Empress" of The Style Invitational, the *Washington Post*'s weekly humor/wordplay contest, every single week from 2003 through 2022, covering all kinds of humor, from cartoon captions to neologisms to elaborate song parodies. She spent twenty-six years as a copy editor and desk chief in the *Post*'s "Style" section, tinkering with other people's writing and writing pun-riddled headlines, plus occasional extracurricular tinkering with other people's book manuscripts. She lives with her husband in the DC suburb of Fort Washington, Maryland, eats everything with the joy and gusto of a golden retriever, and obsessively walks nine miles a day.

Krysia Carmel received her BA from Dartmouth College and a JD from Villanova University. Approaching her third decade practicing law, she attests to the fact that her professional career consists mostly of reading and writing, which is fortunate, given her reading addiction and book hoarding tendencies (both of which she inherited from her father). Her law office serves as a convenient repository for her personal (and professional) library collection. While she has been extensively published, this anthology marks her foray into an entirely different genre.

Pat Pannell is a used-to-be-attorney and an ongoing mom to two fabulous girls who've now made it safely to adulthood (partial credit to their father on that). Long ago, she studied English at Dartmouth College and law at Georgetown University, ultimately finding gainful employment in New York City. Nowadays she resides in Princeton, New Jersey, where she volunteers for various nonprofits and has fun playing drums, attempting art, and treasure-hunting in thrift stores. But Pat is *most* happy when she and her phone are roaming, or while dancing like no one's watching to one thousand favorite songs and enjoying excellent movies and books—including Gina's!

Lynn Peril is the author of three books, including *Pink Think: Becoming a Woman in Many Uneasy Lessons*. Her column, "The Museum of Femoribilia," appears in *BUST* magazine, and she is a frequent contributor to HiLobrow.com. She lives in Oakland, California, with her husband and three cats.

Laura Pope lives in New York City, where she works as a full-time nanny and part-time copywriter. Prior to her childcare and writing careers, Laura was an elementary teacher, ballroom dance instructor, and studio photographer.

Though she will never volunteer to go hiking or bake any type of pastry, Laura does love hosting friends in her sunny backyard garden, listening to heartwarming podcasts while running, and reading poignant novels that reduce her to tears. She routinely rewrites song lyrics to make herself laugh, and she strongly believes in raising children to know they are loved just as they are.

Kylie Ramia was born and raised in San Jose, California, where she spent most of her time either reading at the local Barnes and Noble or writing in her bedroom. At eighteen, she moved east to pursue her bachelor's degree in Management Information Systems and certificate of concentration in Creative Writing at the University of Connecticut. Currently, she's working as a project manager at VMware in Atlanta, Georgia, where she plans to continue writing in her free time. *Fast Fallen Women* includes her debut publication.

Emily Raymond is a librarian and a sometimes writer. One of Gina's former students, she graduated from the University of Connecticut in 2014 with a bachelor's degree in English and a love of creative writing. Realizing her passions for reading, preservation, and access to information were a viable career path, she achieved her master's in Library and Information Science from Southern Connecticut State University in 2021. An only child, she always loved hearing family stories, and is glad to have immortalized one of them in this collection. Emily lives in New Haven, Connecticut, with her partner and several plants.

Jennifer Rizzo has been published in the *Hartford Courant* for her narratives "The Loss of Karlonzo Taylor Is a Loss for Everyone" and "The Only Thing That'll Be Showing Is a Ring." Her piece "Better with Age" was also included in *Fast Funny Women*. She received a bachelor's degree in English and a master's degree in K–12 Special Education from the University of Connecticut and her 092 certification and Sixth Year Degree from Sacred Heart University. Jennifer has served as an adjunct professor at Bay Path University since 2016 and teaches in Vernon, Connecticut. She is devoted to social justice and equity in education and currently lives in Connecticut with her husband, two children, and two dogs.

Heidi Rockefeller has all the dirt, and some-day she might write it all down. She has worked for thirty-five years in her own business, cleaning houses and making her world a little tidier for herself and everyone she holds dear. She lives in Connecticut with her husband of twenty-six years and her two amazing daughters. You will most likely find Heidi with a bit of knitting or out back in the garden as she begins her graduate degree in chaplaincy.

Tammy Cristina Freitas Rose is the very proud daughter of Maria de Fatima Martins de Freitas Rose. Like her mother, she brings creativity and joy to everything she touches—from her dis-tinguished work as a playwright for New York City stages and the Thoreau Society in Concord, Massachusetts, even in her day job as a User Experience Researcher in Technology. Yes, she has put those two

master's degrees to work! She currently runs TranscendentalConcord.com, an online community platform and social media source for history and lit-erature nerds, and soon will be coming out with a book on caretaking, grief, and happy memories.

Joyce Saltman is professor emeritus from South-ern Connecticut State University, where she happily taught teachers of Special Education students for more than forty years. Known as "the Guru of Laugh-ter" and "The Chubby Broad from Brooklyn," she has been giving close to one hundred presentations each year on humor-related topics and donating all the fees to her favorite charities. She is world-famous in Connecticut and South Florida! ☺

Jennifer Scharf is a writer with humor essays published in *McSweeney's*, *Scary Mommy*, *Mamalode*, and more. She has her MA in Media and Visual Arts from Emerson College and has worked on numerous short films and stage productions. Jennifer lives in New Jersey with her family and rescue dog.

Greta Scheibel grew up in Massachusetts and went to the University of Connecticut. She spent her twenties traveling and living abroad, discovering how to fall (and get back up) in foreign footwear. While in Africa she met a handsome Brit on a motorbike. It was not Ewan McGregor. They rode off into the sunset and woke up, sometime later, married with two boys in southern Maine. There, by the sea, she spends her days exploring with her boys and writing about her adventures.

Madiha Shafqat is a Pakistani Muslim-American writer who grew up in Middletown, Connecticut, and, as a kid, never saw someone like her positively represented on-screen. All she saw were bad guys. So she took matters into her own hands and wrote an op-ed in the *Hartford Courant* about her experiences being a Muslim-American woman, after which Middletown's mayor, along with Senator Murphy of Connecticut, named February 29, 2016, "Madiha Shafqat Day." Madiha recently graduated with an MFA in Screenwriting from USC's School of Cinematic Arts and is currently working as a writers' personal assistant on a Netflix television show.

Amy Hartl Sherman is a writer and humorist. She graduated from the University of Illinois, only to take to the skies with American Airlines. Married, mother, retired, and refusing to age gracefully, Amy is proud to be loud, and honored to be part of this series of anthologies.

Joan Seigler Sidney is the writer-in-residence at the University of Connecticut's Center for Judaic Studies and Contemporary Jewish Life. Her published books are *Body of Diminishing Motion: Poems and a Memoir* (CavanKerry), an Eric Hoffer Legacy finalist; *Bereft and Blessed* (AntrimHouse), and *The Way the Past Comes Back* (The Kutenai Press). Her poems and essays have been published in many literary journals and anthologies, including *Fast Funny Women* and

Fast Fierce Women (Woodhall Press), as well *Fast Fallen Women*. Sidney has translated Mireille Gansel's *Maison D'Âme* (*Soul House*), forthcoming from World Poetry Books. Four of these poems appeared in *New Poems in Translation* and were nominated for a Pushcart Prize; others will be published in *The Common*, *Asymptote*, and *Migrations*. Sidney had several essays and poems published in recent *Pure Slush* anthologies and an essay in *Gathering*. Other poems recently appeared in *The Maine Review*, *Here*, and the *Willimantic Chronicle*.

Besides her PhD, Joan holds an MFA from Vermont College of Fine Arts, plus a post-graduate certificate in Writing Picture Books. She's an active member of SCBWI.

Jane Smiley is the author of numerous novels, for adults and young adults, as well as some nonfiction. Her newest novel, *A Dangerous Business*, was published in December 2022. Jane won the Pulitzer Prize for *A Thousand Acres*. She lives in California. Although she has fallen many times, she only broke her wrist once, her ankle once, and her heart once.

Dana Starr writes for *Pajamas All Day* at danastarr.net. Her fiction and nonfiction stories are featured in several anthologies and online publications. She writes women's fiction, humor, and memoir, mostly in her pajamas. She also writes, and sometimes finishes, short stories about zombies and the end of the world. Dana is a recovering copywriter who enjoys international travel. Writing on cruise ships is a favorite activity. When not writing, she gives presentations to groups on a variety of topics, including living with an addict in the family and empowering communication careers for females.

Amy Tan's novels include *The Joy Luck Club*, *The Kitchen God's Wife*, *The Hundred Secret Senses*, *The Bonesetter's Daughter*, *Saving Fish from Drowning*, and *Valley of Amazement*. She is the author of two memoirs, *The Opposite of Fate* and *Where the Past Begins*, and two children's books, *The Moon Lady* and *Sagwa, The Chinese Siamese Cat*. Amy served as co-producer and co-screenwriter for the film adaptation of *The Joy Luck Club* and creative consultant for the PBS television series *Sagwa*. She wrote the libretto for the opera *The Bonesetter's Daughter* and is the subject of the *American Masters* documentary *Amy Tan: Unintended Memoir*. She is an instructor of a *MasterClass* on "Fiction, Memory, and Imagination."

Meredith Tibbetts has worked in the government for the past ten years, and her curriculum vitae includes time as a journalist, social media editor, and public affairs specialist. As a photojournalist, she has photographed the three most recent presidents (one was vice president at the time) and interviewed military leaders and celebrities. She earned a BA in Political Science from the University of Connecticut in 2006 and a master's in Journalism from the University of Illinois in 2008. Meredith, her daughter, and two frisky felines reside in Maryland.

Emily Toth, always a feminist activist, wrote her prizewinning dissertation (Johns Hopkins University) on Kate Chopin. She has spent a lifetime rediscovering, teaching, and celebrating women writers. She has created such courses as "Strong Women in Literature: Tough Cookies," "Food Writing," and "Women's Secrets." Her eleven published books include biographies of Chopin and Grace Metalious, a Civil War novel, and advice books for academics under the persona of "Ms. Mentor." Emily is a professor at Louisiana State University, an online columnist, and a speaker about women's lives, humor, gossip, and imagination. She sings in the Baton Rouge Rock 'n' Roll Chorus.

Deborah Hochman Turvey currently resides in Maplewood, New Jersey, with her husband and three children and within spitting distance of her three sisters and seven nieces and nephews. She is a graduate of the University of Connecticut and has spent her career working in children's literature and as an author/illustrator booking agent. Deborah is especially proud to serve on the Board of Trustees for Planned Parenthood of Metro New Jersey and on the Executive Board of the Jewish Women's Foundation of New Jersey.

Kelsey Tynik is an interdisciplinary sculptor working in Brooklyn, New York, and Storrs, Connecticut. Her work investigates glee and sentimentality realized through material, technique, and play. Kelsey has exhibited in New York, Connecticut, Arkansas, Texas, and California. Her most recent exhibitions were at Collar Works and Hesse Flatow (both in New York) and Ely Center of Contemporary Art (Connecticut). She has been an artist-in-residence at Mass MoCA; Arts, Letters, and Numbers; Vermont Studio Centers; and ChaNorth. Her work has been featured in *Hyperallergic*, *Art Forum*, *Create! Magazine*, the *Coastal Post*, and *I Like Your Work*.

244

 **Hiedi Woods** reignited her passion for writing and joined the San Diego College of Continuing Education Writers Workshop in October 2020. Two of her stories were published in their latest anthology, *The Stories Start Here, Volume 2*. She was also an editor for the creative nonfiction submissions. Previously, Hiedi wrote and edited study guides and playbills for Long Wharf Theatre. She currently plays with numbers at an investment company. When she is not writing or reading, she enjoys hiking and visiting San Diego beaches with her husband and son. Hiedi holds a BA in English from the University of Connecticut.

Mia Yanosy graduated from the University of Connecticut with an English degree in 2021. She was a member of the 2021 Connecticut Poetry Circuit and has had a short story featured in the *Iron Horse Literary Review*.

About the Editor

Photograph by Alexander Grant

Gina Barreca is author of ten books, including the bestselling *They Used to Call Me Snow White But I Drifted*, *Babes in Boyland: A Personal History of Co-Education in the Ivy League*, *Sweet Revenge: The Wicked Delights of Getting Even*, and *It's Not That I'm Bitter, Or How I Learned to Stop Worrying About Visibly Panty Lines and Conquered the World*. Translated into several languages, including Chinese, Japanese, Spanish, German, and Portuguese, she has also edited 17 collections, including *The Penguin Book of Women's Humor* and *The Signet Book of American Humor*. Board of Trustees Distinguished Professor of English Literature at the University of Connecticut, Gina has written regularly for *The New York Times*, *The Chicago Tribune*, *Cosmopolitan*, *Ms*, and *The Chronicle of Education*. Deemed a "feminist humor maven" by *Ms*. and called "smart and funny" by *People* magazine, Gina has appeared, often as a repeat guest, on CNN, TODAY, NPR, OPRAH, and GOOD MORNING AMERICA, and has lectured worldwide on humor, gender, power, and trouble-making. She grew up in Brooklyn, New York but now lives with her husband in Storrs, CT. Go figure.